TALES OF A
TEXAS
GAME WARDEN

WHAT
MY EYES
HAVE SEEN

BENNY RICHARDS

Tales of A TEXAS GAME WARDEN
What My Eyes Have Seen

©2021 Benny Richards

ISBN: 978-0-578-90380-4 (Paperback)
ISBN: 978-0-578-90381-1 (ePub)

Book design and layout: Lighthouse24
Cover photos: Kaitlin Richards

The stories in this book are true firsthand accounts of events that occurred during my career. The people and places are real. However, in order to protect them and their families from further persecution and embarrassment, the names of suspects and violators have been changed.

ABOUT THE AUTHOR

Benny Richards was born and raised in Hunt County, Texas. He spent his youth hunting, fishing, and picking up arrowheads in the fields and rivers in Northeast Texas. These experiences would serve him well as a Texas State Game Warden years later.

A graduate of East Texas State University in Commerce, Texas, Benny used his education to launch a career in law enforcement. He became a police officer in Richardson, Texas, in October 1993.

After a short but successful tour of duty there, he entered the Texas Game Warden Training Center in Austin, Texas, on January 1, 1996. His first duty assignment after graduation was in Delta County. During his game warden career, Benny was stationed in numerous counties, mostly in Northeast Texas, but he served all across Texas on different assignments.

Benny received various awards and commendations throughout his carreer, including being named the Shikar Safari Wildlife Officer of the Year in 2015. His love of storytelling led Benny to publish a weekly column called Furry Tales in his local newspaper.

In addition to his reputation of being one of Texas's finest game wardens, Benny is probably best known for his role in the popular TV show *Lone Star Law* that aired on Animal Planet. Benny makes his home now near the small community of Campbell, Texas.

*This book is dedicated to
the three loves of my life.*

*My wife Kristi and our
children Kaitlin and Erik*

BECAUSE HE RIDES

Late, oh so late,
the country folk on their pillows
safely sleep
because he rides.

Under the moonless, star-filled sky,
the does and their fawns
peacefully graze the green meadows
because he rides.

In the shadows,
the evildoers ponder the fate that might befall them
as they nervously stare out into the night
because he rides.

Through the misty twilight,
accompanied by the lonely howl of the coyote,
traveling along muddy roads all alone,
the game warden...

...he rides.

CONTENTS

PREFACE

I WAS ONCE INVITED to be a guest speaker in a senior government class at the high school in Cooper, Texas. A few minutes into my speech, as I looked across the classroom at some bored faces looking back at me, I asked a question. "Does anyone know what a game warden does?"

A girl on the back row quickly threw up her hand. "You protect the animals from being killed."

Then a young man raised his hand. "You check hunting and fishing licenses."

The girl was wrong. As a game warden, I worked for a state agency that promotes hunting and fishing. For the most part, I was there to help facilitate the harvesting of birds, fish, and game animals as long as it was done ethically and by the rules. My job wasn't to protect animals; it was to manage people through laws.

The young man was right, but just barely. I did check hunting and fishing licenses as a part of my duties, but that was only a small part of my day-to-day responsibilities.

The fact is the duties and responsibilities of a Texas State Game Warden are perhaps the most diverse in all of law enforcement. This is much of the reason why Texas game wardens carry a certain mystique. To begin with, Texas is a large chunk of land. Wardens must patrol the forests of deep

East Texas, across blacklands of the farm country, out to the shortgrass prairies of the Panhandle, and over the desert mountains of the West. Wardens also must navigate thousands of miles of freshwater rivers and lakes, as well as the saltwaters of the Gulf of Mexico. Each different environment carries its own challenges, and an officer must be able to adapt. Texas game wardens patrol in four-wheel-drive trucks, but also boats of all shapes and sizes. They patrol from helicopters; off of ATVs, horses, and bicycles; and on foot.

A lot can happen in a state as large and diverse as Texas. Wardens there are routinely sent into danger to rescue survivors of hurricanes and stand guard in the aftermath of terrible tornadoes. They are sent to patrol the border with Mexico to enforce immigration laws. They stand ready to assist other agencies during riots and mass shootings, like the one that occurred in Dallas in 2016, where five police officers were killed. And yes, there are those hunting and fishing regulations that must be enforced... lots of them. Texas State Game Wardens are state peace officers. They enforce a multitude of laws: wildlife laws, environmental laws, illegal drug laws, and alcoholic beverage laws. They enforce laws concerning family violence, the Texas Penal Code, and on and on. Texas game wardens have always been on the front lines of law enforcement in Texas. Danger is an inherent part of their job. Many game wardens have made the ultimate sacrifice in completing their mission.

Most Texas game wardens work alone much of the time in very rural, out-of-the-way, and unnamed places. It is not uncommon for wardens to find themselves in situations where they are enforcing the law on uncooperative subjects who are armed. They are alone, with no other officers in sight for miles. And, at a hidden deer camp on some ranch at midnight, no one could find them, even if backup was available. This is when training, skill, experience, and luck come in. The skills and knowledge they possess, the conditions that they sometimes work under, and the uniqueness of the state they serve make Texas State Game Wardens an elite group of law enforcement officers.

For a quarter century, I was proud to be one of those game wardens. These are my stories.

CHRIS HAS BEEN SHOT

IT WAS ABOUT FIVE O'CLOCK in the afternoon when I walked through the back door of our house near Caddo Mills, Texas. I had been out checking hunters since early that morning. Kristi had dinner sitting on the table and I was more than ready to dig in. As I took my jacket off and sat down at the dinner table, my cell phone rang. I answered to find Bryan Callihan. What he said floored me.

"Hey man, have you heard about Chris?"

"No... what about Chris?"

"Chris has been shot."

At the sound of these words, I jumped to my feet and reached for my coat. I pulled the phone down long enough to tell Kristi that I had to go and that I would explain later. I was running to my patrol truck as Bryan gave me all the info he could, which was very little. Basically, all he could tell me was that Chris was injured badly somewhere on the Cooper Lake public hunting area and people were looking for him.

I hit the interstate wide open with lights and siren blaring. I had a thousand things going through my mind. Who shot Chris? What was he shot with? Was he able to call for help, or was someone with him? The biggest concern I had was where he was exactly. Bryan was unable to give me any location at all. However, I was confident that if I could get any information at all, I would find him. I knew those woods better than anyone on planet Earth. I didn't know what the situation was, but trying to anticipate any scenario, I started making phone calls to game wardens.

The first call I made was to Warden Steve Stapleton in Van Zandt County. As usual, Steve answered the phone already talking, cracking jokes. I interrupted him and said, "Steve, listen carefully... Chris Fried has been shot near Cooper Lake. I don't know the details but I need you to drop what you're doing and head that way. Also, when we hang up, call two other wardens and tell them what I just told you." Steve said, "OK, I got it." He also said he had a four-wheeler on the trailer already hooked up to his truck. I told him to bring it and hurry. I then called my captain to advise him of what was going on.

It took me a little more than half an hour to make the forty-five-mile trip. Along the way, I had switched my radio over the Delta County channel. I was able to listen to conversations between deputies and figured out that I needed to go to a small ranch owned by a local doctor named Welch. The ranch was very near the north end of the Cooper Lake dam. I was very familiar with it.

When I arrived at the front gate of the ranch, I immediately saw Chris's truck parked across the county road just inside a gate on the public hunting area. Numerous people were standing around, and things were somewhat chaotic. My eyes searched the crowd, looking for any familiar faces. That's when I saw Chris's wife Jamie. I ran to her and asked, "Where is Chris?"

"I don't know, somewhere in these woods," she said, pointing east toward the heavy timber. I told Jamie not to worry, I would find him.

It was now dark as I ran through the gate of the Welch ranch and turned east as hard as I could run. In the distance, I could see the lights of a side-by-side ATV headed up the fence line that separated the ranch and the public hunting area. It didn't take too long to catch up with the ATV. Out of breath, I jumped on the back, assuming the driver had some information and a good idea where he was going. Another three hundred yards and I began to see flashlights shining in the woods. I bailed off the ATV, jumped the fence, and ran to the source of the lights. I wasn't prepared for the circumstances awaiting me.

I saw three men huddled around a large oak tree. When I got there, I recognized all three of them. Howard Crenshaw, a biologist for Texas Parks and Wildlife; Dustin Hunter, a state trooper; and Kip Sontag, whom I had known for years. At the base of the big oak, I saw Chris quietly sitting on the ground. I knelt down beside him. I looked at him eye to eye. "Chris, it's Benny... I'm here... We are going to get you out of here." Chris just nodded his head up and down slowly. He then, in a very low and slow voice, asked me about his wife, Jamie. "I've already talked to her, she's here, don't worry."

At this point, paramedic Tanner Crutcher arrived on the scene with his medic bag. I got out of the way and let Tanner go to work. Kneeling beside him, Tanner used scissors to cut open Chris's shirt. Now we could all see the entry wound to the right side of Chris's chest. There was no exit wound. It was obvious to me this wound was made by a large-caliber rifle round. I knew this was a very serious wound. I was actually amazed Chris was conscious. Not wanting to alarm Chris, I walked away and jerked the cell phone off my duty belt and called Chris's captain, Teri Potts. Teri had just been advised what was going on and started asking me questions. I had to stop her. I told her that Chris needed a helicopter immediately.

It might be a matter of life and death. She told me she would try to get one and call me back when it was on the way.

The next few minutes were very frustrating. I could do nothing but sit next to Chris and monitor him as paramedics worked, trying to stabilize him. He remained extremely quiet as his complexion began to turn alarmingly pale. I noticed Kip, Dustin, and several other men having a conversation nearby. Someone had come up with a plan to drive a flatbed hay truck as near as possible and carry Chris to the truck. I didn't like the plan. I thought the jarring truck ride across bumpy, muddy fields would be more than Chris could take. However, the general consensus was that this was the best plan. I was still anxiously waiting on a call telling me a helicopter was coming.

A few more minutes passed as a flatbed truck arrived and waited fifty yards away on the other side of a barbed wire fence on the "Old Blackwell Ranch." Everyone was getting ready to put the plan into action when my phone rang. Finally... I just knew I was about to hear that a CareFlite helicopter was on its way. Instead, it was Teri calling me back advising me she had been told no helicopter was available to fly because of the weather. "Horse shit!" I was never so pissed in all my life. The weather wasn't bad. There was a thin mist in the air, but damn, this officer's life was hanging in the balance. I was disgusted, but there was no time to argue about it, and no one I could argue with. It was now time to get Chris on that truck as soon as possible and get him out of the woods.

We put Chris on a backboard, but he began to protest immediately. Lying flat on his back caused him severe pain and made it hard to breathe. Most likely his right lung was already collapsed. He sat in an upright position on the board as several men carried him through a hole that had been cut in the fence. They then loaded him onto the truck for the half-mile trip to the highway. I got on the flatbed and sat next to Chris. He was weak, pale, and barely conscious. I said to Chris, "I want you to squeeze my hand every few seconds, OK?" Chris just slowly nodded his head up and down. I put my hand in Chris's hand and the truck started down the field road. The ride wasn't as bad as I thought it would be, but we did encounter one obstacle. A low-water concrete crossing over a steep creek. Climbing up and out of the creek bed was hard on Chris.

Looking ahead, I could see a lot of vehicles at the front gate of the ranch. When we pulled up alongside the waiting ambulance, Chris was rushed inside. Jamie was there waiting for her husband. When she tried to get inside the ambulance to see Chris, she was told she couldn't. That didn't go well for the ambulance staff. Jamie let it be known, with no uncertainty, she was getting inside the ambulance. They backed down and allowed her inside... rightly so.

For the first time in the last hour, I was able to start thinking about something else besides Chris. I looked around and saw numerous game warden trucks. All the wardens were circled around the ambulance, concerned about their friend and teammate inside. I was approached by the wildlife biologist, Howard Crenshaw. Howard was actually the first person to get there after Chris made a call for help from his cell phone. Howard told me that Chris relayed to him that the bullet that struck him was fired from the Old Blackwell Ranch. Upon hearing this, I immediately went into investigation mode.

We were all standing on the Old Blackwell Ranch. That meant that whoever shot Chris might very well still be on the ranch. Howard went on to say that he had been told there was a group of out-of-state hunters who had been hunting on the ranch earlier that day. I looked around at the large crowd of people that had gathered. There was a lot of law enforcement, medical personnel, and just onlookers. Then there was another group of young men gathered a small distance away. I didn't recognize any of them. I yelled to Steve Stapleton and Wood County warden Kurt Kelly, who were at the front gate, "Hey guys, no one goes in or out that gate until y'all get a name and license plate number." They gave me the thumbs-up.

Game Warden Captain Teri Potts, the Delta County sheriff, and a Texas Ranger had arrived by this time and were interviewing the ranch owner. I walked over to speak with them as the ambulance carrying Chris left the property en route to the hospital in Sulphur Springs. The owner, who was being cooperative, confirmed that he had a group of hunters from Illinois staying at the ranch. It was the same group of young men who had been huddled up earlier. Everyone who didn't have a legitimate role to play at the scene was identified and asked to leave. The ranch owner and all his guests were asked to return to the main lodge and wait inside. Most all the game wardens left and travelled to the hospital, where Chris would be fighting for his life. Warden Daniel Roraback and I stayed behind. I was convinced that whoever shot Chris was still present at the ranch and I wanted to get to the bottom of what happened.

After another hour inside the lodge with the sheriff and the ranger, Teri came out and briefed me and Daniel. All the hunters inside the lodge denied any knowledge of what happened to Chris. We were told there were a dozen rifles inside the lodge that needed to be transported to the sheriff's office to be stored until they could be tested against the bullet Chris still had lodged inside his body. Daniel and I collected all the firearms and headed to town. At the sheriff's office, Daniel and I photographed and logged in each rifle as we placed them in the evidence safe. During this process, our department internal affairs investigator, Bradley Chappell, showed up. He was followed by the sheriff, the ranger, and four to five of the hunters from the ranch. They began to separate and interview all the hunters individually. Captain Teri Potts left to go to the hospital.

Daniel and I had been getting frequent updates on Chris. We were told at one point that he was in very critical condition and might lose his left arm from lack of blood flow. The hospital in Sulphur Springs was unable to adequately treat Chris, so he was transported to Parkland Hospital in Dallas. I was later told by game wardens who escorted the ambulance carrying Chris to Dallas that the seventy-five-mile trip was a hair-raising, white-knuckled race at high speed. Back in Delta County, the hunters stuck to their story... "We don't know nothing." It was very late now, so Daniel and I decided to go home, get some sleep, and return to the ranch at daylight. Chris was in surgery.

The next morning, I got started just as the sun was coming up. I drove to the Old Blackwell Ranch. I waited there for Daniel and our internal affairs investigators to show up. I passed the time snooping around the area where we had loaded Chris on the truck. I noticed fresh four-wheeler tracks in a nearby field. The tracks led to a barn several hundred yards away. I followed the tracks to the barn. Entering the barn, I could see mud on steps leading up into a loft. Up inside the loft, I observed a chair sitting in front of the loft window. Next to the chair, on the floor, were numerous cigarette butts. The view from the loft window afforded a clear line of sight to the spot where Chris was standing when he was struck by a bullet.

11

Daniel showed up and met me outside the barn. We walked a straight line from just below the loft window toward the spot where Chris fell. Our walk took us to the fence line that separated the ranch from the public hunting area. Hanging on the fence there was one of the yellow boundary markers that identified the property as public hunting land. The yellow sign had a perfect round hole through it. It was an obvious bullet hole. I jumped the fence and walked to the spot where Chris was hit. Daniel peered through the bullet hole and found me standing approximately fifty yards away. After lining me and the hole up, he noticed a small brush pile between the two. While examining the brush, sharp-eyed Daniel located a hole through a sapling. Here again, it was an obvious bullet hole. So now we had some evidence of what might have happened. But without being able to talk to Chris, we couldn't confirm our suspicions. Brad Chappell and another IA investigator showed up finally and we showed them what we had found. We assisted in photographing the area and then we left. Daniel and I had done all we could do.

Chris, against all odds, survived his gunshot wound. The .308-caliber bullet damaged his lungs and cut an artery before lodging in his left armpit. News that Chris had survived and was about to start telling his story caused two of the hunters' lips to start moving. One of them had shot Chris from the barn on the ranch. He claimed he had shot at a boundary sign. They claimed it was an accident and they had no idea Chris had been injured. Chris told a different story. He claimed he yelled at the two hunters after being struck by the bullet, but they got on a four-wheeler and drove away. Regardless, the physical evidence showed that, most likely, a bullet fired from the barn travelled about four hundred yards before passing through a metal sign, then through a two-inch sapling, before striking

Chris. Talk about being at the wrong place at the wrong time. Chris finally recovered from his injury and went back to work. In the years that followed, Chris Fried became my closest and most trusted game warden partner.

CRITTER, CRITTER

SEPTEMBER WAS ALWAYS A TIME OF TRANSITION for me as a game warden. In mid-September, I was usually putting those long days on the lake in the rearview mirror and looking forward down the road to the hunting seasons quickly approaching. Dove season was open and archery season only a few weeks away. Brutally hot Texas days were giving way to cooler mornings and afternoons. The change in seasons have always caused hunters to start stirring. When hunters start stirring, good game wardens do the same.

One September night just after dark, I was sitting around the house, bored to death. There was a bright full moon outside and I felt like I needed to be working. There's something about a full moon that makes people do strange things. If anything was going to happen on this night, I wanted to be a witness to it. Apparently, I wasn't the only warden suffering from this restlessness. About nine o'clock, the phone rang. It was Delta County Game Warden Chris Fried on the line.

"Hey man, have you seen the moon outside? Let's go see if we can get into something."

The invitation was more than I could resist. We agreed to meet at the police station in Commerce, Texas. Chris climbed in the truck with me and off into the night we went. There have been very few occasions when Chris Fried and I worked together at night that we didn't run onto something interesting or illegal. This night would be no different.

By midnight, we had run up and down numerous dirt roads through some of my prime honey holes without any luck. It was beginning to look like we had jumped the gun by beginning our night patrols a couple of weeks too early. Working our way back toward Commerce, I was searching my own brain for historical data that would lead us in the right direction. Then I remembered a lonely dirt road that cut through the Middle Sulphur River bottoms. The prior hunting season, I had received several complaints about spotlighting in the area, so we decided to give it a shot.

As we turned off of Highway 11 onto the county road, Chris was in the middle of bringing me up to speed on Delta County gossip when I interrupted him suddenly. "Did you see that... did you see that?" Pointing east to the horizon, I said those magic words, "Q-Beam." Now there was complete silence as I blacked out all my lights and went into stealth mode. No words were necessary, as Chris and I had been in this situation many times before. We both knew what to expect and what our roles would be... or at least we thought so.

I used the light of the moon to navigate the dusty road as we closed in on our prey. My imagination conjured up images of a couple of good ole boys with a spotlight and a .22 out for a nocturnal deer hunt. As I slowly rounded a curve in the road, there they were. About two hundred yards ahead, stopped in the middle of the road, was a pickup truck blacked out except for its amber fog lights and red taillights. I killed the engine on our patrol truck and Chris and I got out. We had no more than gotten still and quiet when we clearly heard laughter... loud female laughter. Puzzled, Chris and I looked at each other over the hood of the truck. The laughter continued, interrupted intermittently by a high-pitched squeal. My theory of hunters pursuing trophy whitetails was quickly fading. We kept listening intently, hoping to hear something that would give us some clue as to what was going on in the middle of that country road just ahead of us. Chris and I were like racehorses in the starting gate when we heard doors shutting. Then the truck suddenly started. We jumped back in our ride, started up, and began to follow.

Chris, who has much more patience than I do, wanted to continue to follow the truck through the bottom to see what happened next. I, on the other hand, had seen and heard enough and wanted to stop the truck immediately. Since it was my truck and I was driving, we implemented my plan. I closed the gap between the two vehicles to fifty feet before throwing all my lights on. Headlights, red and blue lights, takedowns, everything all at once. The truck continued on as if nothing had happened. Now I was thinking, "We're about to have an old-fashioned car chase." I reached down and hit the air horn a couple of times, which brought the suspect truck to a complete stop in the middle of the road.

Exiting the patrol truck, Chris and I walked forward. I was on the driver's side... he was on the passenger's side. Arriving at the driver's-side window, I shined my flashlight into the cab, where I saw two young men and a young lady. The first young man, the driver, was shirtless and shoeless, wearing only a pair of unbuttoned jeans. The second young man, seated next to the passenger door, was wearing only underwear. The young lady, seated in the middle... only a thong. Further examination of the cab revealed the evidence I was looking for. A big yellow spotlight was lying in the floorboard. But... where was the rifle?

I asked the driver to get out. Chris asked the other guy to get out. I took the driver to the front of the truck for discussion as Chris took his guy to the back. I began my questioning by asking the tall, burly fellow what he was using the spotlight for. He just shrugged his shoulders and in a booming voice said, "We ain't been shining a spotlight." I assured him that I had clearly seen a spotlight working right where his truck had been previously parked in the middle of the road and that any further denials about shining a spotlight would fall on deaf ears. About then, Chris walked up, shaking his head, and said, "I can't get nothing out of that guy." There was no rifle in the truck and searching my twenty-plus years of experience for clues, I was stumped at what I was seeing. What explained the laughter that we had previously heard? Why were these people less than half dressed? What about the spotlight? These were questions I was asking myself.

Finally, I said, "Boy... do you want to tell me what's really going on here?" Hanging his head, he began to speak.

"Well, sir we were playing Critter, Critter."

Intrigued, but still confused, I said, "Do you want to explain to me what Critter, Critter is, son?"

He replied, "Well, when it gets dark you all get in a truck and drive through the country. You use a spotlight to look for animals... you know, their eyes... The first person to see the animal's eyes yells, 'Critter, Critter!' and they win. The other people have to take off a piece of clothes."

Upon hearing this, Chris turned to the open truck door and shined his flashlight on the girl sitting nervously in the truck. He said, "Well, from the looks of her, those animals sure must be moving tonight!"

At this point, I was having a hard time keeping a straight face. We wrapped up our investigation rather quickly and sent the trio on their way. Watching the red taillights disappear in the distance, I thought to myself... how great would it be to be a teenager again?

COLD, HARD RAIN

VERY OFTEN, people I would meet as I traveled around the countryside would ask, "What's the scariest thing you've ever seen as a game warden?" I always had a very quick answer ready.

It all started on a stormy night in Delta County in the fall of 1999. Late one evening, I got a call from Lamar County Game Warden Darla Barr, asking for assistance at the "Kensing Crossing" on the North Sulphur River. The Kensing Crossing is a concrete low-water crossing between the Kensing community in Delta County and the Cunningham community in Lamar County. Darla explained four teenagers had gotten into a flat-bottom boat earlier in the day at the Highway 24 bridge and were attempting to float the river downstream. She said it had been reported to her that they had no motor, no paddles, and perhaps no life jackets.

I knew immediately that this was a bad situation. It had been raining hard off and on for two days and the river was up about two feet. The North Sulphur River between Lamar County and Delta County is a man-made channel that took the place of the old original riverbed. It was dug in the 1930s to help stop flooding back then. It's long and straight and when it's full, the river runs fast, very fast.

I arrived at the south bank of the river with my flat-bottom boat just after dark, followed by my new partner Sean Reneau. On the opposite side were two Lamar County wardens, Darla Barr and Bryan Callihan, along with several sheriff's deputies. No one had seen or heard from the missing teens for several hours.

Then came the rain. A cold, hard rain like I had never seen before. Communicating with the wardens on the opposite side of the river was impossible due to the roaring sound of the rushing water and the pouring rain. The water rushing over the concrete crossing had formed a waterfall with about a three-foot drop and a strong undertow on the downriver side. Sean began untying ropes that were holding down my boat to my trailer.

I asked, "What are you doing?"

He replied, "Getting ready to unload. We're going to look for them, aren't we?"

"No, it's too late for that. We're going to wait for them right here."

Agitated, he said, "We can't wait, we have to go up the river."

"Look, Sean, one of two things has happened: those kids have gotten out of the river and are walking to the nearest light they see, or their boat flipped and there's nothing we can do for them right now."

My words fell on deaf ears. I had lived near the North Sulphur River all my life and I knew better than to challenge it under those conditions. Sean, on the other hand, was new to the county and unfamiliar with the river, but he was about to get a firsthand lesson. Sean was beside himself and his frustration was beginning to turn into anger. I finally gave in and agreed to launch my boat into the river. The last thing I told him before backing the boat trailer to the river's edge was, "I just want to go on record as saying this is a really, really bad idea."

As the boat slid off the trailer into the murky water, the current immediately grabbed it and swept it quickly downstream. Sean, who had wrapped the bowline around his wrist, was jerked off his feet and pulled into the river. I was yelling at him at the top of my lungs to let go of the rope as I grabbed his gun belt and pulled him back toward the shore. I guess Sean could see he was fighting a losing battle because he did indeed turn loose. All we could do at this point was stand helplessly and watch my boat race towards a waterfall that was growing bigger by the second. Like something out of a horror movie, the boat stood straight up on its end and then was tossed over to the other side of the river like a toy. Everything in the boat was thrown in the water. Gas tank, battery, life jackets, flashlights—everything was lost.

Bryan slogged down the muddy riverbank on the other side and was able to get hold of the bow line and tie it to a four-wheeler. Together, the wardens and deputies were able to turn the boat over and pull it into a small cove that had formed on the other side of the river. I figured this large dose of reality would dampen Sean's eagerness to go up the river. Nope... he grabbed a rope out of his truck and began trying to throw it across the river to Bryan and the deputies on the other side. After three or four attempts, he finally got the rope across and it was tied off to the rear bumper of Bryan's truck at the edge of the water. Sean and I shucked our gun belts and started across the river, using the rope to pull ourselves along the concrete crossing only two feet from the raging waterfall. It took all our strength to hold onto the rope and cross against the rushing water that was thigh deep and rising quickly.

Once on the other side, we regrouped and began transferring parts from Darla's boat, still on the trailer, down to my boat. At this point, Bryan put on a life jacket and asked me, "Do you want me to go too?" I actually did want him to go. There was not a better warden to have in the boat with you during an emergency than Bryan Callihan. However, three grown men in the boat in those conditions would have been a gamble. If we did find the four teenagers and have to load them in with the three of us, it would have been a disaster. I asked Bryan to stay on the bank just in case we got into trouble and needed him there.

In the few minutes it took to get the motor running, the river had already come up another foot. Ten yards upstream of the waterfall, Sean pushed us away from the bank and I throttled up the forty-horsepower motor against the current. On the opposite bank, Hoyt Kennemer, a good friend and nearby landowner, yelled to us, "Be careful!" I appreciated Hoyt's concern for sure, but we were way beyond trying to be careful. This river trip was going to be survival of the fittest.

We headed up the river into the darkness, using only a flashlight to see by. Sean used his flashlight to search the riverbank on both sides for any signs of the kids. We had traveled a half mile or so when Sean yelled, "I see something coming!" His light was centered on a white object floating down the middle of the river toward us. Within seconds it hit the side of our boat like a torpedo. It appeared to be an old water heater that someone had probably dumped upstream weeks, maybe months before. Sean's flashlight ran down quickly, so I gave him my small backup light. It lasted about five minutes and then it was dead. Now we were completely in the dark with a hard rain falling, and the river continuing to rise.

About this time, my pager went off for the first time. These were the days before wardens carried cell phones. I ignored the pager and we pressed on upriver. Suddenly, the prop struck something under the water and the motor died. As I frantically tried to restart the motor, our flat bottom turned sideways and we were drifting at the mercy of the river. The current pushed us to the river's edge and alongside a large log. Sean, sitting on the bow of the boat, used his feet to push us away from the log. I finally restarted the motor and got us back out into the center of the river. My pager went off again, and again I ignored it. Sean, without much success, began trying to bail water out of the boat using his hands cupped together. Our situation was pretty dire. We had not seen any sign of the teenagers we were looking for, and it was now that I started thinking of my own wife and kids. I really wanted to see them again.

I told Sean, "We have done all we can do. This ain't working." Sean nodded in agreement as I pointed the boat back downstream and headed back. Then my pager went off again. This time I pulled it out of my pocket and saw Darla's call number, 8206, followed by 911. I knew then Darla was trying to send us a message, but I didn't know what it was. It didn't take long to get back to the crossing. As we got close, I could see Hoyt again. He was standing on the south bank with a flashlight and a rope. As we went by, riding the current, Hoyt threw Sean the rope. It was tied to his four-wheeler. Hoyt then got on the four-wheeler and tried to pull our boat out of the river. The current was so strong that Hoyt stripped several gears pulling the boat, but he got us out. Sean and I jumped out and tied the boat to the boat trailer. We were both thankful to be alive.

Now Darla yelled across the river that the teenagers had been located. It turned out that soon after we left, headed upriver in the boat, a man called the sheriff's department advising that he had four lost teenagers at his farmhouse. Seems the kids we were looking for had abandoned their boat when it got dark and the river started rising. They then walked across muddy fields to the first light they saw. I hate to say that I was right... but... I was right. Anyway, I was just happy to be back on solid ground. I gave Sean a big bear hug and together we loaded the boat on the trailer. Then all the wardens and deputies got out of that muddy bottom as fast as our four-wheel-drive trucks could take us.

That night, Mother Nature reminded us all that she's in charge. I also had a lot of respect for my new partner after that night. Sean Reneau had a lot of heart and not an ounce of quit in him. Two very good qualities that I like to see in a partner. Looking back on it, that ordeal on the North Sulphur River that rainy night was the scariest thing that ever happened to me as a game warden.

HE'S IN THE TRUCK

AFTER A LONG SLOW NIGHT patrolling along the river in northern Red River County, I decided to head to the house and call it a night. I was headed south on Highway 410 just north of Detroit, Texas, when something caught my attention.

In an oak grove to my right, I could see the red glow of brake lights. I brought my patrol truck to an immediate stop beside the highway. I wondered what in the world anybody would be doing at two o'clock in the morning on this secluded ranch. I came to the conclusion, based on many, many years of experience, that someone was trying to kill a deer behind the game warden's back. I parked my truck, hopped the barbed wire fence onto the ranch, and headed up the hill toward the red lights.

As I started the half-mile walk, I heard two distinct rifle shots and observed a spotlight working in the woods. I entered the oak grove and quietly walked to within one hundred feet of the vehicle before I crouched down behind a large tree stump. Looking and listening, I observed two men outside of a pickup truck. Sure enough, one of the numbskulls was dragging a deer. He dragged the deer up to the truck but did not load it.

At this point, both men got into the truck on the passenger side. I heard the truck's engine start and then it began moving in a large circle through the trees. A spotlight was being used out the passenger side. The truck continued in the circle until it was now driving directly toward me only fifty yards away. Suddenly, I saw a deer run between me and the approaching truck. I'm sure I was holding my breath as I heard the truck stop and the squeak of a door opening. I fell flat and hugged the ground out of fear of what I was afraid would be next.

A spotlight locked onto something to my right in the thick woods. Seconds later, the crack of a rifle shot broke the silence. Now, I overheard a conversation between two men concerning a deer and looking for blood. I continued to lie flat against the earth as the two nighttime deer hunters walked in circles just yards from where I lay motionless. They finally gave up and got back into the truck. After shutting the passenger side door, the truck once again cranked up and once again out came the spotlight.

As the truck drove past me, I made my move. I sprang from the ground, jumped up on the rear bumper, and hung onto the tailgate. I could now see there were three men inside, oblivious to the new passenger they had just unknowingly picked up. I rode along for a short distance before I decided I had seen and heard enough. I pulled the flashlight from my gun belt and shined it through the open sliding glass behind the center of the passenger seat and yelled at the top of my lungs, "Game warden, stop the truck!" At the sound of my voice, I heard someone inside the cab yelling to the driver, "Go, go, go!" Instead, the truck came to an abrupt stop. Again I heard someone yell, "Go, go, go!" Another voice interrupted, saying, "He can't go anywhere, dumbass, he is in our truck."

I stepped off the rear bumper, made my way around to the driver's side of the truck, and ordered everyone out. The pistol I was holding let everyone know I meant business. After gathering up the three men's driver's licenses, I asked the men what they had been shooting at. I guess the driver was betting that I had just showed up because he said they had been shooting at hogs. As the drunk driver was choking on his lies, I could see one of the other drunk men had blood on his hands and pants. I confronted them about it, but they continued to insist it was hog blood. "Oh, really?" Pointing at the tree line in front of the truck, I asked, "If we were to go over there, think we might find a dead hog?"

Now all three fell silent. I removed two rifles and a spotlight out of the truck and told them, "Follow me." I walked about thirty yards to a dead doe that had her throat cut and was partially covered with leaves. Sarcastically, I said, "Hmmmm… fellas, that don't look like a dead hog to me, so let's cut the crap." I looked around the area but could not find a second deer that I was confident had been shot. I advised the three men that they were under arrest, but I had a little bit of a situation. My truck was parked a half mile away and I had no backup. Because they were heavily intoxicated, none of these guys were in any shape to drive their truck. I locked their truck and took the keys. I then handcuffed the three men together and, pointing toward the highway, I said, "Get to walking."

On the trip back to my truck, I radioed to the Red River County sheriff's office and asked them to send me a couple of deputies to help me transport my suspects to the jail. When we finally arrived back at my truck, there were two deputies waiting. As I began unhandcuffing my suspects and sending them through the barbed wire fence, one of the deputies started laughing and said, "This looks like something out of an old western movie." We took them to jail.

Early the next morning, I returned to the ranch and, in the daylight, I was able to find a small yearling buck that had been shot. Cutting into the animal, I was able to retrieve a bullet. I now had all the evidence I needed to prove who had shot it. I returned to my office in Clarksville and filed all the necessary paperwork to charge the three men with hunting deer at night, and a laundry list of lesser charges. The three stooges all eventually pled guilty.

LITTLE BLUE EYES

DO YOU BELIEVE IN premonitions or paranormal activities? I never did put much stock in that stuff, but every now and then in this life something will happen that will make a person wonder. Once, I investigated a strange incident that could have come right out of *The X-Files*. When stationed in Red River County, I was very rarely at the regional parks and wildlife office in Mount Pleasant. I tried to avoid that place.

One August afternoon I was there, turning in my monthly paperwork. I was talking to one of the office ladies when the phone rang next to her and interrupted our conversation. She picked up the phone and answered, "Hello, Texas Parks and Wildlife, this is Amber, how can I help you?" A minute or so later I could tell by the puzzled look on her face that this was no ordinary caller on the line. My interest perked up even more when she said, "It just so happens, the Red River County game warden is standing right here... Let me let you speak to him."

This was my first clue that something out of the ordinary was going on. I mean, what were the chances of someone calling the regional office looking for the Red River County game warden and I would be standing right next to the phone?

Amber turned to me and, with a crooked grin, she rolled her eyes and handed me the phone, as if to say, "Get ready for this one." Anyway, when I answered, a very upset woman on the other end began to hysterically tell me that a little girl was about to drown in the Red River. "Whoa there, lady." I then asked, "Who are you, where are you, and what little girl?" She never slowed down, and described the little girl as blue eyed, blond haired, about eight years old, wearing a white shirt. After every little bit of information, she would say, "We have to stop this!" Trying to figure out what was going on, and where, I asked her, "Is she in the river now?" With her voice cracking and full of emotion, she said, "Not yet."

Now I was really confused. Next, she really threw me a curve ball. She told me she was a psychic. She then claimed she was having constant visions of a little girl drowning in the Red River. At this point, I wanted to put her on hold long enough to look up the phone number for the state hospital for the mentally ill. I continued to listen intently and decided this was not a prank call. This woman was for real and truly believed everything she was telling me. The woman was emphatic when she asked If there were any long bridges over the Red River in my county. She claimed, in her visions, the little girl was near a long bridge, screaming and waving for help as the current was pushing her under. In another attempt to convince me of her sincerity, she advised me that she was truly a psychic and had helped law enforcement solve crimes on several occasions in the past.

I put aside my doubts long enough to confirm to her that yes, there was indeed a long bridge over the Red River that I knew of. She began to beg and plead with me to quickly drive to the river and save the little girl from drowning. I agreed to make the trip up north to have a look. I thought this was all hogwash and she was crazy, but, what the heck, I didn't have a whole lot to do that afternoon anyway. Just to prove to myself that I wasn't buying into all of this, I didn't get into any hurry. I even stopped to get a drink and a candy bar in Clarksville, and then headed to the river. When I arrived, I got out of my truck and walked underneath the Highway 37 bridge, where I found nothing. I walked to the edge of the river and looked down into the muddy current as a few tree limbs floated by. A few yards away, I could see small whirlpools forming around the concrete bridge pillars. I thought to myself, "That's the last place I would want to drown." Walking back up on top of the bridge, I looked east and I looked west… There were no signs of anyone drowning, fishing, or doing anything else. "Well, this is what I figured… waste of gas." I called my psychic contact back to break the news to her. She urged me to keep looking, but I finally told her, "I think I've done all that I can do." That should have been the end of it, but it wasn't.

A week or so later, I happened to be up in the north end of the county checking on an injured owl that had been reported to me. The owl turned out not to be injured, but instead he was dead when I got there. Since I was up in that area already, I decided to drive over to the river bridge. As I approached the bridge, something caught my eye on the Oklahoma side of the river. It was children swimming. Odd…. I didn't ever see kids swimming in that muddy river. I pulled over to the side of the road and, using my binoculars, I took a closer look. What I saw almost caused me to fall out of my truck.

Three little girls, about eight years old, were swimming near the opposite shore, and one was blond haired, wearing a white T-shirt. I could feel chill bumps running up my spine.

As I raced across the bridge, I saw two adult women sitting on the edge of the riverbank. I pulled off the roadway onto an old four-wheeler trail in order to get down to the river. Upon seeing my patrol truck approaching through the willows, the women began calling the girls to the shore. I guess they thought they were in trouble or something. The little girls had gotten out of the water when I pulled up.

I sat quietly in my truck as the women dried off the girls and began loading up their things in a minivan. I left without speaking a word to them. I drove all the way home, wondering if some divine intervention had taken place.

I guess no one will ever know.

LAST FLIGHT TO TEXAS

IT WAS A WARM NIGHT for October. I broke a sweat setting up the two "stuffed" hogs in a small field beside the secluded dirt road east of Cuthand, Texas. Daniel Roraback and I were on night patrol in Red River County. We had a camera crew riding with us from the popular TV show *Lone Star Law*. We wanted to catch a night hunter red-handed and get it on film. Daniel and I decided the best option for doing that was putting out some bait and giving a poacher something to shoot at. The area we were set up at was a well-known hotspot for illegal night hunting. As we waited, hidden in a small grove of trees on the north side of the road, the two fake hogs stood silently on the south side, waiting to stop a bullet.

We had been there about 30 minutes when Daniel's cell phone rang. The Red River County sheriff's office was on the line. The dispatcher advised a small airplane had been reported missing. She also stated the plane was owned by one of our favorite landowners in the north end of the county… Buck Hill. Daniel got off the phone with the county and immediately called Buck. Buck was in Florida at the time. Upon answering the phone, Buck relayed as much limited information as he could to Daniel. He told my partner that his son, Dylan, was flying the plane. He also said the plane, which left the small Idabel, Oklahoma, airport about six thirty in the

TALES OF A TEXAS GAME WARDEN

evening had actually been spotted preparing to land at his ranch but never sat down on the grass airstrip there. Daniel tried to comfort Buck by giving him our assurance that we were going to find the plane and his twenty-four-year-old son.

We loaded up everything and headed north. The plane we were looking for was a single-engine Aviat Husky. The pilot was a really good kid Daniel and I had both known for a number of years. This made it all the more important to us that we find that plane and that boy.

We arrived at the ranch headquarters at about 9:00 p.m. A couple of sheriff's deputies and some volunteer firemen arrived about the same time. Dylan's girlfriend met us in the driveway. She told an interesting story about waving to him as Dylan flew low over the main lodge and banked the airplane. She assumed he was getting ready to land so she went back inside. Dylan never showed up at the lodge. An hour passed before she started getting worried and began calling his cell phone. After not getting any answer to her repeated calls to his phone, she started calling family members to report Dylan missing.

After listening to her story, I came up with two scenarios. One was hopeful. The other not so much. Perhaps Dylan had forgotten something back across the river in Idabel and simply flew back to Oklahoma. That's what we hoped for. However, the possibility that his plane had problems and went down loomed large in our minds. At any rate, we tried to stay positive. I got on the phone to law enforcement in Idabel, who were already looking for the plane at the municipal airport there. Daniel got on the phone with his brother Josh, who was a state trooper. Josh arranged to have a Department of Public Safety helicopter meet us.

In the hour that passed before the helicopter arrived, Daniel and I got a map and drew a straight line from Idabel to the lodge on Buck's ranch. We figured if the plane had gone down it would be along that line on the map. That entire area of Red River County was heavily forested. Without an exact location, looking for anything in those big woods at night would be futile.

More county deputies, volunteer firemen, state troopers, and Game Warden Bryan Callihan showed up. A command post was set up at the end of a county road between the Red River and the north end of the Hill Ranch. Law enforcement in Oklahoma reported back that they had not been able to locate our missing plane. In the distance we could hear it coming, the rhythmic beat of an approaching helicopter. Once it was overhead, Daniel got on the radio and made contact with the DPS pilot. After being briefed on the details, the pilot started at the main lodge on the ranch and slowly began searching the probable route Dylan had taken. A large spotlight was used to peer down through the thick canopy of treetops. At the command post there was complete silence and all eyes were on the helicopter as it methodically worked back and forth in a grid pattern.

Twenty minutes passed by before I noticed the helicopter began to make small circles. It then lowered just above the treetops, shining its spotlight in one spot. The silence was broken when the pilot's voice came over the radio. "What color is the plane?" Daniel replied, "Yellow." Then we heard the words we didn't want to hear. "I've found it, just below me." Lake racehorses coming out of the gate, Daniel, Bryan, and I jumped in our four-wheel-drive patrol trucks, along with the *Lone Star Law* camera crew. All the patrol cars had to stay behind because of the rough terrain.

Using cow trails, utility right-of-ways, and thin spots in the timber, we made our way to the downed plane. Once I had the helicopter hovering just above me, I stopped the truck and Daniel and I bailed out. We ran through the heavy timber to the spotlight beam just ahead. We were hoping to find Dylan alive, most likely injured, but alive.

As I got to the plane, I stopped and used my flashlight to inspect the wreckage. My worst fears were right in front of me. It was immediately obvious that Dylan was no longer of this earth. He had not survived. The plane was a twisted mass. I then turned and walked to the camera crew, who were coming quickly through the heavy timber. "Turn the cameras off." I told them not to film this. Out of respect for the Dylan and the rest of the Hill family, I wanted him to leave this earth with his dignity intact.

As the helicopter flew away, other rescue personnel started showing up on foot. Who knows what caused his plane to go down? Dylan ended up about a quarter mile short of the grass runway on the ranch. This event was hard on every one of us that knew Buck and his son. However, the hardest part was still to come.

Daniel, Bryan, and I drove back to the lodge, where much of the family was, waiting for word. We delivered the terrible news. Then, Daniel had the unthinkable task of calling Buck and telling him about his son. Of all the death notifications I was involved in, this one was by far the most uncomfortable.

COUNTRY AND WESTERN DEER HUNTING

LAKE CREEK, TEXAS, is a tiny community in the north part of Delta County. A lot of hunting was always going on up there in the fall. Some of it was on the shady side.

One evening I stuck up my deer decoy in a wheat field along the highway. I had no more gotten it set up and gotten hidden in the ditch on the other side of the pavement when a small pickup came along, driving very slowly. As the truck got closer, I could hear the radio thumping out a country and western tune. When the truck rounded the curve, the two teenage boys inside spotted the decoy and slammed on the brakes right in front of me, thirty feet away.

When the truck stopped, I saw the fellow in the passenger seat get up on his knees and stick a rifle out of the window. The driver's side window was also rolled down, so I could hear everything that was about to be said inside. After a long pause, the would-be shooter said, "I can't hold it still." The driver encouraged him by saying, "Shoot, shoot, he's going to run!" Another long pause went by before the shooter asked, "Why ain't he moving?"

At this point, I stood up and quickly walked to the driver's side window without the boys ever knowing I was there. A short argument broke out between the two over whether or not to shoot.

Finally, I leaned inside the window and said, "Go ahead and take a shot, let's see what happens."

The sound of my voice caused both of them to almost jump out of their skins. They both spun around, looked at me, and began stuttering. After a quick and thorough scolding, I sent the boys on their way.

Over the next few years, I was around those two boys quite a bit, but I never had any more problems with them road hunting—or anything else for that matter.

BATTLE ON THE RED

MY EARS PERKED UP when Daniel mentioned that name. He was working on a deer case that started when he got a tip from an informant. "Seems this guy doesn't know deer season is over." Daniel then showed me a cell phone picture of a deer that had been killed a few days earlier. "Do you know a guy named Jerry Lee Burton?"

I said, "Hell, yes I know him... What did he do this time?"

Jerry Lee was well known to me and most other law enforcement officers in Red River and Lamar Counties. I had arrested him before and issued him numerous citations over the years. In my opinion he was a loathsome individual. Jerry Lee hadn't been on my radar for a couple of years, so I was very interested in his latest violation of the law. Apparently Jerry Lee had shot a nice buck deer and was sending his friends pictures to brag a little. The problem was he didn't have a hunting license and deer season was over. The pictures ended up in Daniel's hands. So Daniel and I decided to pay Jerry Lee a visit at his cabin.

Trying to find Jerry Lee was not always an easy task. If he knew you were coming, he would hide. If you did manage to find him, he would likely run. Our plan was to wait until late at night and catch him in bed. Before heading out we did a computer check and found out he had two active warrants for

TALES OF A TEXAS GAME WARDEN

his arrest. One felony warrant for a violent incident between him and a state trooper over in Lamar County, in which he fled and escaped. This information made things a bit more serious.

Just before midnight, we arrived at the front gate to his property and, surprisingly, it was unlocked. Daniel blacked out the lights and we drove in. We slowly rolled past Danny's house… Jerry Lee's brother… and continued on. Jerry Lee's cabin sat right on the bank of the Red River in a very secluded location. Once we arrived, we put our plan into gear.

Jerry Lee and I knew each other very well. I was afraid if he looked out the window and saw me he would never come to the front door. However, Jerry Lee didn't know Daniel, so if he went to the front door there was a chance of getting him outside. I was wearing my heavy ballistic vest and carrying my M4 rifle. I wasn't going to take any chances with this man. I hid behind a large tree at the corner of the cabin. Daniel walked to the front door and knocked. I was amazed when the door suddenly opened and Jerry Lee strolled outside to meet Daniel, who had backed up several yards.

Unsure if this was our guy, Daniel asked, "Is Jerry Lee here?"

The reply came without hesitation, "Nope he went to town."

Jerry Lee, as usual, was again lying to the police. He then asked Daniel, "Who are you?"

"I'm Daniel Roraback… I'm a state game warden."

Jerry Lee turned three shades of pale at this point. Concerned that he might attempt to run back inside the cabin, I quietly slipped out from behind the tree and walked to the door. Once I had his escape route cut off, I felt a lot more confident that we had him.

We now had him surrounded and he was unaware of my presence. Daniel started firing questions at Jerry Lee to distract him as I walked up behind him. Once in place right behind him, I spoke up.

"Jerry Lee, you are under arrest."

As he turned to face me, I reached out and grabbed a handful of the T-shirt he was wearing. Jerry Lee took one look at me and began violently struggling to get away. Holding my M4 rifle in my right hand, I was in no position to subdue him. In less than two seconds, he had torn out of his shirt and started running toward the river. Daniel was right on his heels as they ran down the steep riverbank and out of sight.

An additional problem suddenly showed up. Jerry Lee's pit bull exited the cabin and joined the chase. As I hit the riverbed, I could see Daniel's flashlight dancing in the distance as he gave chase down a long sandbar. I didn't know how long it would take, but I was certain Daniel was going to catch him. Loaded down, I did the best I could to keep up.

The foot chase lasted for about two hundred yards before Daniel nabbed him as he tried to run up and out of the river. A struggle ensued. When I caught up to the grown men fighting halfway up the riverbank, I could hear Daniel yelling the commands he had been trained to say in the academy, from which he had only recently graduated. "Stop resisting… police… you are under arrest!" Those types of commands bounced off Jerry Lee like water off a duck's back.

I unshouldered the fully automatic M4 rifle and laid it on the ground at the bottom of the riverbank and then joined the fight. Daniel had managed to get one handcuff on Jerry Lee before he was severely head-butted. I ended up hanging onto the loose handcuff. Jerry Lee was fighting us like a wild animal now.

Daniel pulled out his pepper spray and gave him a good blast to the face, but I got sprayed too, in my left eye. Our problem in controlling this guy was we had to adhere to rules.

Only the minimum amount of force could be used to make the arrest. On the other hand, Jerry Lee wasn't playing by any rule book. The pepper spray didn't have any effect on him, so I told Daniel to choke him out as I held on to the dangling handcuff. Daniel sprang upon him and applied a choke hold.

Jerry Lee began to scream at the top of his lungs. "Danny... Danny... help me Danny!" He was trying to recruit his brother up above to come to his rescue. Great... just one more thing we had to worry about.

The chokehold Daniel had applied began to take effect. Jerry Lee got quiet but continued to resist arrest. I began to worry that after being pepper sprayed and all the physical exertion, he might be permanently injured. Hoping that we could now get him handcuffed completely, I told Daniel to stop. I was totally wrong in thinking that he was ready to give up. Jerry Lee took a big breath and started fighting us harder than ever. I somehow ended up on the bottom of the pile. Then in the darkness two things happened.

I heard a growl and then realized Jerry Lee's dog was trying to bite my neck. Thankfully, my ballistic vest protected me. The dog only had a mouthful of fabric and Kevlar. With pepper spray in one eye, lying flat on my back using both hands to control one loose handcuff, I couldn't move. I became aware of movement near my pistol holster. Using my elbow, I could feel a hand dangerously close to my weapon. This situation was totally out of control now.

Jerry Lee somehow managed to stand up and use his foot against a willow tree to push off of. This caused the three of us and a dog to begin tumbling down the riverbank. We all ended up rolling around on top of my M4 rifle. After a brief scuffle there, Jerry Lee broke free and ran toward the water. I gave chase and regained control of the loose handcuff. Standing face to face, Jerry Lee used his free hand to grab me by the throat. Daniel responded by using his ASP baton to begin striking Jerry Lee's legs. Without results, Daniel moved up and began delivering strikes across his arm. Jerry Lee's pit bull responded by biting Daniel's legs. Daniel pulled his pistol and fired near the dog causing it to back off.

I had seen enough. This was now a fight for survival. I thought if this went on any longer someone was going to get seriously hurt or killed. It was past time to bring this terrible situation to an end.

I told Daniel to stand back. I let go of the loose cuff and then Jerry Lee and I had a fight… a serious fistfight. He lost badly.

After that, Daniel and I were able to get him on the ground and complete the handcuffing. This brought it all to an end. The entire ordeal that started on his doorstep and ended two hundred yards away lasted about seven minutes.

We summoned an ambulance to the scene to decontaminate Jerry Lee and myself from the effects of pepper spray. Daniel also had dog bites and a big goose egg on his forehead that needed attention. Then a sheriff's deputy transported Jerry Lee to the Red River County jailhouse in Clarksville. Numerous charges were filed against him, in addition to the charges that were already pending. During an interview at the jail, Jerry Lee confessed to having killed a deer. The next day, Daniel and I returned and retrieved the head of a whitetail buck off the roof of Jerry Lee's cabin.

In the end, it was obvious that Jerry Lee didn't learn a damn thing. In the years following our arrest of him, he was involved in several more incidents with local law enforcement. Some people never learn.

DOG GONE

I WALKED AWAY from the deer camp thinking… these guys are going to get themselves in trouble tonight. Thirty minutes earlier I was attracted to the camp by the sound of constant gunfire. Four fellows from Dallas had decided to drive out to the country for a weekend of hunting and drinking. They came well armed with four Bushmaster assault rifles and four handguns, along with hundreds of rounds of ammo. They had set up camp in an old barn just off Highway 410 near the Rugby community in Red River County. When I was in the camp checking hunting licenses, I inquired about the quarry the hunters had planned on pursuing. "Deer, hogs, varmints, anything really," came the reply, and then laughter. I laughed as well, all the way to my cell phone that I used to call my partner, Daniel Roraback. I told Daniel not to plan anything for that night because we had work to do. I gave Daniel a few of the details and he was all ears.

About eleven o'clock that night Daniel and I returned to the area and I backed into a hiding spot on a high hill about a quarter mile from the camp. We didn't have to wait very long. After only a few minutes we could see the bright beam of a spotlight working the tree line behind the old barn. As we watched the spotlight in the distance something began rustling in the brush beside my driver's-side window. A dog had showed up. Stepping out of my patrol truck, I could see this wasn't a bad-looking hound. I told Daniel he might have some beagle in him. As I petted the pooch on the top of the head, he wagged his tail and put on his very best "I'm a friendly dog, please take me home" act. The poor thing was probably dumped by someone a few days earlier and had not eaten anything for a while.

At this point, the hunters in the distance decided to make a move. We could clearly see they had driven out of a field onto Highway 410 headed north, shining the pastures along the roadway. The thing to do now was circle around front and intercept them. We bid the little dog farewell and wished him luck as we drove away into the dark. Following the maze of narrow blackland roads, we finally hit FM 411 and then drove with our lights out to the intersection at Highway 410. However, once we got there we discovered they had made a U-turn and were now headed back south. We were still blacked out when we finally caught up with them. We followed and watched as they worked spotlights out both sides of the big Ford four-door truck. Two miles later, wouldn't you know it, they turned onto the same dirt road that Daniel and I had been previously hiding on and watching from.

We continued to follow about one hundred yards off their back bumper. Rounding an S curve, the truck stopped suddenly and a beam of light coming from the driver's side of the truck locked on to something in the ditch. The poor little homeless dog showed up again looking for a new home at the wrong place and the wrong time. Before we could have done anything to prevent it, two rifles were pointed out the side windows and they cut the helpless animal down. Unbelievably, the driver of the truck got out and pumped a couple more rounds into the dog with a pistol. It was a bad night to be a dog with these morons in town. Now, very pissed off at what we had just witnessed, we followed them for a few more minutes up the road. They did another U-turn only to be met with our red and blue lights blocking the road in front of them.

Daniel got all four of the men out of the truck and I lined them up shoulder to shoulder in the middle of the road. I suppose they had no idea we had been following them. When I asked what they were doing, the big fat driver said, "Just riding around."

I then asked, "What are y'all looking for with those big lights?"

He said, "Hogs. They are causing damage."

Daniel spoke up, asking, "Did y'all shoot anything?"

"Nope." Upon hearing this lie, I decided to have some fun. The following conversation then took place.

Me: "Guys, me and this other game warden came out here looking for my dog that I lost this afternoon. We saw y'all's lights and came to see what was going on."

When I mentioned a dog, all four men dropped their heads, and began staring at the ground while fidgeting.

Me: "You guys haven't seen a little white-and-black dog with brown spots, have you?"

Them: "No, sir."

Me: "I ask because my neighbor told me earlier that he had seen my dog hanging around back near that corner in the road... Sure you haven't seen him?"

Them: "No, we haven't seen a dog."

Me: "Are you guys absolutely, positively certain you haven't seen him? I need to find him because he means a lot to my family."

In complete silence, all four men just stood there shaking their heads side to side.

Me: "Ok… well, if y'all haven't seen my dog, would one of you please tell me what the hell y'all were shooting at a few minutes ago?"

Surely all of them must have been close to shitting their pants now. With his lips quivering wildly, the ringleader spoke up and said, "Sir, we are very sorry but if we had known it was your dog, we wouldn't have done it, I promise."

Having now exposed them as the liars and idiots they were, Daniel and I got down to business. Two of the men who had not fired a gun were allowed to drive the truck back to camp in order to avoid towing it. The driver and his partner in crime were arrested, taken to jail, and charged with numerous violations. That turned out to be one expensive mutt.

FARMING IN THE CITY

A GAME WARDEN isn't usually looking for a dope case when one falls into his lap. Such was the case for me late one night in Delta County. I was sitting in my truck hidden in some trees at the John's Creek boat ramp. A few knuckleheads around Cooper were bad about driving down the road that led to the ramp, shining a light all the way in an attempt to snipe a deer. I was hoping to catch one of them red-handed.

About 11:00 p.m. a white pickup slowly came up the road and drove to the middle of the parking lot at the ramp. I never saw him shine a light, so at first I wasn't too concerned. The truck came to a stop and a young man stepped out. He walked to the rear of the truck and set a beer can down on the bumper. He then unzipped his pants and began to take a leak, unaware anyone was around. Using my binoculars, I noticed he was swaying a little bit as he took care of his business. After finishing up he grabbed the can of beer, tilted his head back, and guzzled the last swallow. Throwing the can on the ground, he then headed back to the driver's seat. Drunk drivers are dangerous and this guy showed signs of being plastered. I decided the night hunters would have to wait.

I flipped on my lights and came out of my hiding spot. I got out of my patrol truck and confronted the guy at his door. As it turned out the guy was drunk, very drunk. However, he had two other more serious problems. I found numerous illegal drugs hidden in his truck, including marijuana, ecstasy, and prescription pain pills. He also had a loaded pistol under the seat. I gave the guy his Miranda warning and off to jail we went.

At the jail, as I was busy doing paperwork, my arrestee kept asking how much trouble he was in. I informed him more than once he was in quite a bit of trouble. While all this was going on the chief deputy, who had been listening, began to heckle the guy about going to prison. The word *prison* caused him to turn white as a sheet. My suspect then began to make me a very strange offer that went something like this: "If I can tell you where some more drugs are, will you cut me a break?" Of course, I wanted to know what kind of drugs and how much. He was very vague but assured me and the chief deputy he could lead us to more drugs.

After a brief discussion with the chief deputy I explained to the guy that if he led us to more drugs I would consider dropping some of his charges, as long as the district attorney approved. I also explained to him that I was making no promises, and everything he was about to say and do was voluntary. He took the deal.

As we left the jail with several deputies in tow, I asked the chief deputy to call the sheriff and advise him of what was going on. We were directed to drive to a small frame house in a neighborhood only four blocks from the sheriff's office. Basically, we were in downtown Cooper. At the house my guy stopped us at the front door and said, "Now, everything in here is mine... None of it is my roommate's stuff... It's all mine, OK?"

He opened the front door and led us inside. As soon as I walked through the door I could smell the odor of burnt marijuana. On a coffee table in the living room sat a big glass bong and rolling papers. The deputies quickly found a small bag of marijuana lying on the couch. We were led into my guy's bedroom, where he handed the chief deputy a shoebox that held several bags of marijuana inside. We noticed the individual bags had his initials written in black ink on them. In an adjacent bedroom another deputy discovered the roommate fast asleep. Wouldn't you know it? There were several bags of marijuana on the nightstand next to his bed in plain view. Guess whose initials were on those bags? The roommate was now under arrest also.

As the deputies rummaged about, collecting evidence, I wandered into the kitchen and noticed something strange. I saw three extension cords running from outlets in the kitchen under the back door of the house. When I brought my guy into the kitchen and asked about the electrical cords, he turned white as a sheet for a second time. I think this guy had expected us to have wrapped up our investigation back at the bedroom. He tried to explain that the cords just simply ran shop lights out in the shed.

I followed the cords out the back door to a wooden shed in the back yard. I threw back a black tarp that covered the doorway. I noticed foam insulation had been stuffed around the door for some unapparent reason. When I opened the door I was almost blinded by the intense white light coming from inside. When I stepped inside the shed I'm sure my mouth fell open as I stared in amazement at what I discovered. I found out later on an internet search that it was called a hydroponic marijuana growing operation. It was the most elaborate weed growing operation I had ever seen at that point in my career. Dozens upon dozens of marijuana plants were suspended from the ceiling. Pumps circulated water from tubs on the floor up to the top of holding trays where it flowed down to the plants. Ultraviolet lights took the place of sunlight. The Delta County deputies spent the rest of the night dismantling the operation and photographing the evidence.

The next day I was in sort of a pickle. I had uncovered a major drug supply operation in the heart of a small town where I was raising my children. I wanted someone to pay. However, a deal was a deal. True to my word, I cut the guy a break, and he answered to lesser charges than he could have faced. I didn't feel too bad about it. The operation was shut down, we took away the dope, and the two potheads left town soon after

FORD vs CHEVY

ONE NIGHT IN LATE SEPTEMBER of 2008 I decided to head out to the Blackland Prairie west of Bogata, Texas, to see if I could catch a night hunter killing deer. About 11:00 p.m. I backed into my hiding spot next to an oil field pump jack on a high hill overlooking the farmland a mile in every direction. For over an hour I sat patiently waiting, dozing off occasionally. Just after midnight, I saw the glow of headlights approaching a slight S curve in the dirt road a half mile west of me. Then a vehicle appeared, slowly headed in my direction. Suddenly the vehicle stopped and blacked out in the middle of the road. I knew something was up so I grabbed my binoculars and stepped outside my Ford patrol truck for a better look.

A minute or two went by before I saw the beam of a flashlight move away from the truck and into a small patch of woods next to the road. At this point I didn't know what was going on but figured somebody was about to go to jail for something. This oil field area had been hit several times recently by copper thieves and it was a well-used area for nighttime deer hunters. A little voice told me I should get some help headed my direction, just in case whoever was driving this vehicle decided to run.

Taking my own advice, I called the Red River County dispatcher over the radio to ask for assistance. Usually whenever I called for assistance late at night, every deputy in the county would come running because they knew it was going to be something good. This time was going to be no different. Deputies Briggle and Cobb responded, along with Bogata officer Bell. Over the radio I explained to the officers what was going on and asked Briggle to block County Road 1200 at Highway 410. I instructed Cobb to block the intersection at Highway 37 and stand by. I now decided to get a little closer to my suspect in order to find out what he was doing.

With my headlights turned off, I slowly drove out onto the county road and eased toward him. After I closed the distance to a quarter mile, I stopped and got back out of my truck. Standing in the road, I again saw the beam of the flashlight move away from the vehicle and into the woods for the second time. One minute later, I saw the light return to the vehicle and then go out. Everything was quiet for a few moments. Then I could hear a slight rattling noise, which got progressively louder. I threw up my binoculars and looked down the road.

"Holy crap!" In the dim moonlight I could see a white truck driving up the road toward me with no lights, only one hundred yards away. I quickly jumped back in my truck and got ready. When the truck got closer I could finally see him approaching in the darkness. When the truck was less than thirty yards in front of me I flipped on every light I had… red and blues, spotlight, takedowns, everything. All my lights illuminated the inside of his cab like the Fourth of July. I could clearly see the scraggly looking white guy who was driving and the surprised look on his face. It didn't take long for me to figure out that this guy didn't want to talk to me and had no intentions of stopping. He shifted into reverse, threw his left elbow out on the edge of the driver's door, stuck his head out the window looking backward, and the chase was on.

I grabbed the microphone off the hook and told the deputies, "He's running, you guys come on." This guy was running from me in reverse and I figured this was going to be a very short chase. I could not have been more wrong. I followed him at about forty miles per hour with my front grill guard about ten feet from his front bumper. My spotlights were blinding him and he was having a hard time keeping his truck on the road. When I turned on the siren it startled him, which caused him to lose control and end up in the ditch. If it had been muddy that night the chase would have been over right there, but because it had been so bone dry, he was able to get back on the road and continue running.

As we entered the S curve, I deployed my secret weapon. I hit my airhorn and it scared the living shit out of the guy. I saw him jump, almost hitting his head on the ceiling before he went into the ditch again. After getting back on the road, he began weaving through the curve. In the distance, I could see Deputy Briggle closing in from the west. In my rearview mirror, I could see two sets of red and blues coming. I guess the runner saw Briggle too. Coming out of the end of the curve he purposely backed into the ditch.

I stopped in the road with my vehicle canted to the left in a defensive posture. Deputy Cobb slid to a stop on the edge of the road to my right and bailed out with his handgun drawn. Trying to anticipate his next move, I stayed in my truck, closely watching the suspect. He took one look at Deputy Cobb and me blocking the road and, without hesitation, shifted into drive and floored it. I did likewise and got out of his way. His truck jumped back onto the road and passed between my rig and Cobb's patrol car, slinging dirt in every direction. The last time I saw Cobb, he was standing between our two units, pointing his pistol, yelling at the man to stop. As I did a quick U-turn in the cornfield to my left, I wasn't sure if Cobb had just been run over and killed.

Things were now very serious. I got back in the chase with a whole different mindset. The suspect was no longer running backward. He was driving forward, without lights, very fast. The 1985 Chevy pickup he was driving had four on the floor and was more than capable of leaving me in his dust. I grabbed the radio and tried to call Cobb to see if he was hurt, but he didn't answer. I assumed the worst. I did hear Briggle and Bell saying something about damage to a patrol car. I found out later Bell, who had also arrived in a hurry, had run into the front of Briggle's car in the confusion, causing some front-end damage.

I pursued the suspect down County Road 1200 to Highway 37. At 37 we turned north for a couple of miles before he turned off on another county road. It was very hard to stay close to the guy because of all the dust he was stirring up behind him. I had to hang back a little, just in case he lost control and stopped suddenly in front of me. I pursued him through a maze of county roads. He almost lost it a couple of times, and so did I. Eventually, he headed down a long straightaway, which allowed me to close in on him.

Suddenly out of the dust, a body came flying out from underneath his vehicle. I slammed on the brakes but it was too late. I hit it with the right side of my grill guard. It took a couple of seconds for it to register what had just happened. He had struck a deer, rolled it under his truck, and slung it into me. I was really pissed off now. The chase made a big circle and unbelievably ended up back on the road where it had all started. As my runner was headed up the road toward

Highway 410, I decided I wasn't going to let him get back on the pavement. I still wasn't sure if he had injured Officer Cobb, but I decided he was clearly a danger to society and needed to be stopped, one way or the other. My plan was to plant my grill guard onto his back bumper as he turned onto the highway. However, that never became necessary.

About one hundred yards before the intersection, white smoke started boiling out from underneath his hood. The old Chevy had been pushed a little too hard and the engine was blown. As the truck slowly rolled to a stop, the suspect inside stuck his left arm out the window as if to give up. I jumped out and began yelling at him to throw his keys out the window. He didn't say or do anything, he just sat staring straight ahead with his arm out the window. As I got close to the driver's-side window, I holstered my pistol and reached through to grab a handful of hair. As I pulled his head out the window with one hand, I reached in and tried to open the door with the other. The suspect rotated between grabbing my wrist to prevent me from opening the door and grabbing the steering wheel to prevent me from pulling him out the driver's window. About that time a patrol car pulled up and to my relief out jumped Officer Cobb, alive and well. After Cobb assisted me in removing the suspect from his truck, I handcuffed the bad guy as he lay face down in the dirt road. I gave him a good cussing, and that put an official end to the chase.

As it turned out, he really was a bad guy. A records search revealed that he had just recently gotten out of prison. Of course, now he was on his way back. I never did figure out why the guy started running in the first place. If it was something inside the truck that he didn't want me to find... a gun... or drugs... he must have thrown it out during the pursuit. I did come up with a theory. He had four really nice Weed Eaters lying in the bed of his truck when I got him stopped. If a person were to steal four Weed Eaters and hide them in the woods, it would take that person two trips into the woods to retrieve them, which is what I had observed. He probably had stolen the equipment, hidden it, and returned to get it when I jumped him. But that was never proven.

In the end, I had caught someone killing a deer at night. It just didn't go down quite like I thought it would.

GHOST BUSTIN'

As a game warden I travel a lot in the backcountry. I often see interesting things and occasionally meet interesting people.

One stormy night, back when I was stationed in the Texas Panhandle, my partners and I had pulled off of Lake Meredith due to the weather. With all the severe thunderstorms hanging around we decided to call it a night and I headed to the house. I left Dumas about midnight on my way to Dalhart, forty-five minutes away. I decided to take the backroads home to shorten the drive.

The country between Dumas and Dalhart is a very desolate and uninhabited place, littered with the remains of farmhouses that were abandoned during the great Dust Bowl days of the thirties and fifties. It was one of those abandoned farmhouses that caught my attention as I passed by it on a lonely dirt road. As I whizzed by the front of the house at fifty miles per hour, I caught a glimpse of a white light coming from inside. I immediately knew something was up, for I was familiar with this abandoned house and there was no reason for anyone to be inside that place at midnight.

Turning around, I turned off my headlights and very slowly drove back. Stopping in the road near the old house, I noticed two vehicles parked at the back. My first thought was, "Uh-oh, here we go again... illegal drug activity." I didn't know what was going on at this point, but I assumed the worst. I was a long, long way from any help so I decided to call the sheriff's office and ask for assistance from a deputy just in case things went downhill.

I leaned the seat back and began the wait for the deputy to arrive. However, just a couple minutes later two men and two women came out of the back of the house carrying lanterns. I drove around to the back of the house, blocked the two vehicles in, and got out. I confronted the group and asked the obvious question, "Whatchyall doin'?"

One of the women answered, "We are trying to make contact with the spirits of this house."

"Come again?"

One of the men, sensing my confusion, said, "We are trying to get pictures of any ghosts around here."

At this point, I didn't know whether to pull my pistol or bust out laughing. The looks on their faces and the expensive cameras hanging around their necks let me know these fruit loops weren't kidding. I was very leery of these folks due to the heavy black makeup both the men and the women were wearing around their eyes and the all-black attire they were dressed in. Not letting my guard down just yet, I took a quick tour around the cars and inside the house.

Inside the house I found several sound recorders and motion sensors set up on tripods. This was very expensive equipment that you don't see every day. Interested in the workings of the stuff, I asked one of the women, "Well, did y'all find anything?"

Sensing that I may have taken an interest, her eyes opened wide and she excitedly said, "Yes, we did… listen to this." She then turned on one of the recorders and everyone suddenly got quiet. Trying to be open minded, I listened very carefully for a few seconds, but all I could hear was my brain telling me that I was in a room full of kooks.

About that time I heard the sliding of gravel and knew the deputy had just arrived. I went outside and began to explain to him about the wannabe ghost busters. After I had finished, without any change of expression on his face, the old deputy walked over to the group and began enthusiastically telling them about a very haunted house that he had personal experience with. In great detail he explained that it was just over the county line near Stratford. He even drew them a map of how to get there.

The group was now giddy with excitement as they loaded up their gear and tore out toward Stratford. After they had disappeared over the horizon in a cloud of dust, I turned to the old deputy and asked him to tell me more about the haunted house. He laughed out loud and said, "Hell, boy, there ain't no haunted house in Stratford, but it'll take them the rest of the night to figure that out, and in the meantime, they won't be in our county."

Obviously, this wasn't that deputy's first rodeo. A wise man he was.

HE'S GOT A GUN

IN LATE OCTOBER BACK IN 2006 Warden Rick Lane and I were at it again. Our latest search for a night hunter had taken us up to the north end of Red River County, about three miles south of the Red River, the border with Oklahoma. We stopped for about fifteen minutes at a roadside rest area watching for spotlights along Highway 37 before we pulled out of our hiding spot to head farther north.

As soon as I turned onto the highway, Rick and I saw a vehicle approaching a half mile ahead of us. Unexpectedly, the vehicle made a right turn onto a lonely dirt road and disappeared. I say unexpectedly because it was two o'clock in the morning, and that particular road only had three houses on it. What could be going on down there at that time of night? After a brief discussion, Rick and I both came to the conclusion that somebody was up to something that needed checking out by two veteran game wardens. We happily volunteered.

I turned off my headlights and hurried along to catch up with our suspicious vehicle. As I turned off the highway onto County Road 2349, we encountered the vehicle, a small compact car, stopped in the center of the road. The driver of the car was shining a flashlight out the window into the woods. A couple of seconds went by before the driver took his foot off the brake and slowly proceeded down the dark, rutted road. Our hunch was right: we were following a night hunter and deer meat was on his late-night menu.

The driver slowly made his way down the road, swinging his headlights back and forth across the ditches into the woods every one hundred yards or so. Every now and then the driver would use his flashlight to closely inspect something beside the road. Driving slowly, I hung back a little ways, watching and waiting. We followed the poacher for about a mile before he made another unexpected turn.

The car swerved into the drive of one of the only houses on the road. After stopping in the driveway, the driver turned off his headlights, shifted into reverse, and backed out on the road facing us. Caught off guard, with no time to hide, all we could do was sit in the middle of the road and wait as the suspect car rolled toward us with its lights out.

"Well, Rick, I guess this is it… You ready?"

"Yeah," he said, "light 'em up."

I flipped on my headlights and the red and blues. As soon as I did, the driver of the other car turned on his headlights and punched it. It was now obvious he had no intention of stopping and was going to make a run for it. In response, I jerked the steering wheel to the left and blocked the road as best I could. He raced up to the front of my vehicle with two wheels on the road and two wheels in the ditch. The ruts in the ditch were too deep for his little car to go around me so he was forced to stop with his front bumper one foot from my grill guard. Now it was on. Rick bailed out on his side as I bailed out on mine and retreated to the back of the truck. Once behind the tailgate, I pulled my pistol, spun around, and got ready for a fight.

Kneeling down behind my rear bumper, I leaned around and lit the interior of the car up with my flashlight. I could see two men in the front seats. I yelled at the top of my voice, "Show me your hands!" The driver—who, by the way, was one of the funkiest looking humans I ever saw—immediately threw up his hands. My attention then became centered on the passenger. He was staring at me with a grimacing look on his face. His left arm was down by his side. His right arm was hanging out the open window beside the car.

It was at this moment that I gave all the credit to God Almighty for protecting me. He protected me by giving me very keen instincts... and he also gave me Rick Lane. I instinctively knew that this guy had something in his hand that he did not want me to see. I was ready for whatever it was. Twice more I yelled, "Show me your hands... dammit, you better show me your hands!" I got absolutely no response to my commands. The guy just sat there, very still, staring straight ahead.

Meanwhile, Rick had carefully made his way around behind the suspect's car. At this point I'm sure they were not aware of Rick's presence. I kept my sights trained on the suspect's chest as, out of the corner of my eye, I saw Rick rounding the back of their car. "He's got a gun!" Rick yelled out the warning to me as he pinned the man's arm to the outside of the car door. Once Rick had the fool in his grasp, it was over for him and out the window he went. Rick handcuffed him and took him to the center of the dirt road where he "helped" him sit down. I got the driver out and handcuffed him as well and sat him down next to his partner in crime. There they sat, Dumb and Dumber.

Walking around the car, I saw the weapon the man had dropped on the ground. It was an old military-style bolt-action rifle, sawed off at both ends. I picked it up and examined it and then realized the man had been planning to ambush me and make a widow and orphans out of my wife and children. I was some kind of pissed when I came back around the car. I wanted to bitch-slap the weasel but I got control of my anger.

"Rick, have you searched them yet?"

He shook his head. "Not yet."

I pulled the driver to his feet and checked his pockets. As I was searching him, he was constantly mumbling incoherently and fidgeting. He was also blinking his eyes quickly and biting his bottom lip. The guy only had maybe two teeth left in his mouth, and they both looked like pieces of candy corn. He had scabs all over his face and arms. All of these were sure signs of serious drug abuse.

When it came time to search the passenger he wouldn't stand up so I stretched him out in the road and began rolling him over like a log, checking his pockets. In his jeans pocket I found a handful of 9 mm pistol ammo. "Hey where's the pistol, dude?" He shrugged his shoulders and told me there was no pistol. "Don't give me that crap... a man don't carry pistol bullets unless he's got a pistol." He then clammed up and refused to say another word. Rick and I searched the vehicle, trying to find a hidden pistol. We never located a pistol but, to our surprise, we did find all the ingredients needed to cook methamphetamine, along with hundreds of prescription pain pills.

When all was said and done, we got the two bad guys to the jail, where they were charged with a laundry list of things. A records search revealed that both guys were felons from Oklahoma and both had recently been released from prison in that state.

Looking back, that was one of the most dangerous situations I had been in at that point in my career. Those two felons knew when they saw my red and blue lights they were going back to prison, unless they could get around me and run back to Oklahoma. At least one of the men in the car was ready to kill me in order to make an escape. I never ever wanted to shoot another human, so I'm glad he never raised his gun. If he had, a later autopsy would have shown that he died from a hail of bullets coming from my pistol. Anyway, Rick and I made it home safe again.

A THANKSGIVING TO REMEMBER

ONE THANKSGIVING AFTERNOON I was working the deer decoy on a friend's property near Cooper, Texas, in an area where I had been getting a lot of complaints about road hunting. I had the decoy set up in a grassy field across a dirt road from me. This was a good area where deer liked to cross. The problem with the area was it was very open and there were not many places to hide my truck. I ended up hiding my truck behind a barn about eighty yards away from the decoy. This did not allow me to actually watch the decoy. My plan was to use my ears more than my eyes to alert me to approaching vehicles.

I spent the afternoon sitting in the front seat of my truck listening to the Dallas Cowboys football game on the radio. Every thirty minutes or so I would get out and look around the barn to check on my bait. Each time there he was, standing tall and strong, an open invitation to any would-be poacher. I sat that afternoon and listened to the entire football game and, to my disbelief, did not see a single vehicle come by for over three hours. At the conclusion of the game I got out of the truck to stretch my legs. After that I walked to the corner of the barn to check on things.

As I looked around the barn I was shocked to see a good whitetail buck running up a trail from the road right toward me. What really stunned me was not the size of the buck, but rather it was what he was doing. He was bucking up and down like a bull in a rodeo. I had never seen a wild deer act like that. Anyway, I headed over to my truck to get my trusty rifle with plans on bagging a Thanksgiving Day buck. After grabbing my rifle out of the back seat I headed back around the barn. I rounded the corner just in time to see the buck run around the other side. I reversed course and ran around to the opposite side as well. I again encountered the crazy buck. He was jumping up and down, swinging his head and rack wildly, side to side. I found him in the scope and squeezed off a round, striking him solidly in the chest. The big deer stumbled but turned around and headed for a fence through thick brush. I wasn't able to get off another shot before he crashed into the barbed wire, which threw him to the ground. The buck pulled himself to his feet, sailed over the top wire, and disappeared into the brush.

Feeling confident in my shot placement, I walked over to where he jumped over the fence but found no blood at all. After five minutes or so of looking, I never found a blood trail. However, I did find a small piece of bone about the size of a thumbnail on the ground by the fence. Frustrated, I decided to load everything up and go get help with tracking the wounded deer before dark. This is about the time I got the biggest surprise of all. When I walked across the dirt road to pick up the deer decoy, I looked up to discover it was gone. Unconcerned at first, I figured the wind had blown it over. That was not the case. I located my prize deer decoy lying in several pieces on the ground. Head over there, leg over here, Styrofoam scattered everywhere.

It now became clear to me what had happened. The buck I had just shot had only one minute earlier given my decoy a severe ass whipping. He enjoyed it so much I guess it caused him to lose his mind. He celebrated by bucking and kicking up his hooves. His short celebration ended when I showed up with a rifle.

After it was all said and done, I lost my decoy and the big buck both. I searched the woods for two days and never found him. After that afternoon I never set my deer decoy in a spot where I couldn't see it at all times.

HIDDEN DANGER

BOAT WORK WAS NEVER SOMETHING I was fond of as a game warden. It was cold and wet in the winter and hot and sweaty in the summer. Plus, it seemed like something was always breaking down. The worst part of working out of a boat, however, was the unknown. You really never knew what was lurking just under the water. I found this out the hard way one summer afternoon in 1997.

That summer had been very dry and the water level at Cooper Lake had quickly dropped several feet. On that day I decided to launch my fourteen-foot flat-bottom boat at the John's Creek ramp and patrol the far west end of the lake. After putting the boat in the water, I headed west down the shoreline through the thick, standing, dead timber. I finally found the entrance to boat lane number three and turned south. When the Corps of Engineers constructed Cooper Lake, they cut six boat lanes through the heavy timber in order to provide access by boat to the west end of the lake. At this point, I was straddling the back bench seat while operating the tiller drive of the Johnson twenty-five-horsepower motor with my right hand. I had run down lane number three wide open a hundred times before and I planned to do the same on that day. I gave the tiller a full clockwise turn and wound the engine out. I was buzzing down the thirty-foot-wide boat lane

TALES OF A TEXAS GAME WARDEN

checking out the dead trees, birds, and the occasional dead fish that floated by. I didn't have a care in the world. Then it happened... *BAM!!!*

In the blink of an eye the tiller handle was violently jerked from my hand and the propeller came spinning out of the water. The cowling was slung off the top of the motor, and it sailed out into the water in the middle of the boat lane. My boat swerved hard left toward the dead timber and, before I could brace myself, crashed head-on into a huge oak tree. The violent collision sent me airborne right down the center of the boat. I slammed into the old oak, shoulder first, then fell into the water between the tree and the front of my boat. While all this was going on, a big six-inch-thick limb broke out of the top of the dead oak and came falling down across the bow of my boat. If it had fallen on me, I have no doubt I would have been seriously injured.

Turned out I had hit a submerged stump at full speed. Good thing I was wearing my life vest and a kill switch. I got the breath knocked out of me and my whole body hurt from my shoulder to my knees. I bobbed around a few seconds before I swam back to my boat and pulled myself back in. After putting everything back together, I was amazed when the motor started right up. However, I soon discovered I had spun the prop and wouldn't be using the outboard motor to get back to the dock. I found a long limb hanging from another dead tree nearby and broke it off. I used it as a push pole and started the long journey back.

Over an hour later, I was still pushing when a bass fishing rig pulled up and a fisherman offered me a tow. After that day, I got a lot of comments about the unique inverted "V" nose my flat-bottom sported. Boat accidents such as the one I had on Cooper Lake are not that uncommon and have taken the lives of several Texas game wardens, including Bruce Hill and Barry Decker on Lake Murvaul in 1990. Over twenty years after my accident, Game Warden Zak Benge had a boat accident on the Neches River that was identical to mine, with the exception that he struck something as he flew out of the boat, causing a very serious leg injury that could have cost him his life.

I learned two things from my episode. No matter how well you think you know a lake, never take anything for granted, and never leave the ramp without a paddle.

Cadet Richards navigates the obstacle course at the
Texas Game Warden Training Academy, June 1996.

A good buck deer confiscated from night hunting
poachers just after midnight. (Cooper, Texas)

Not everything that comes out of a lake is a fish. Recovery of a stolen vehicle that was submerged in the city lake. (Hunt County, Texas)

A team of wardens using body drags to search for a drowning victim on Lake Tawakoni. (Hunt County, Texas)

Richards and Roraback take a break during filming of the popular T.V. series *Lone Star Law*. Two hours later the wardens would be on the scene of a fatal plane crash. (Red River County, Texas)

Packing out stalks of marijuana from a public hunting area near the Sulphur River. 12,000 six foot tall plants were destroyed. (Bowie County, Texas)

Wardens, along with K-9 deputy Chris Mars, display a portion of narcotics seized during a traffic stop of a taxi cab warden Richards made on Interstate 30 at midnight. (Franklin County, Texas)

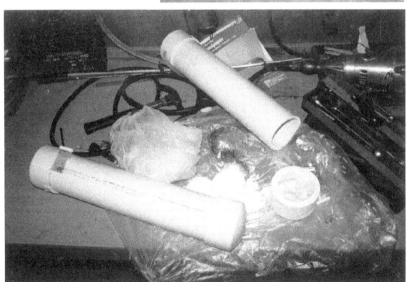

Powdered cocaine packed inside PVC pipe taken from the trunk of a taxi cab. Numerous bundles of marijuana were also uncovered. (Franklin County, Texas)

Looking for survivors in the rubble left behind after by a devastating EF-4 tornado the day after Christmas 2015. (Garland, Texas)

Game wardens search the brush for a suspect that fled a traffic stop during a border patrol operation. A Department of Public Safety helicopter hovers overhead. (Rio Grande City, Texas)

Warden Richards pauses for a photo during foot patrol along the Rio Grande River in 100 degree heat. A human smuggler or "coyote" was arrested later in the day. (McAllen, Texas)

Standing guard above the river. Extremely rough terrain and desert heat in far West Texas was hard on equipment and hard on wardens. (Terlingua, Texas)

Carcass of a deer dumped near the wardens' driveway as retaliation. The culprits were apprehended due to a sales receipt they unknowingly left behind. (Delta County, Texas)

A small yearling buck poachers killed with the aid of a spotlight the previous night. The warden was standing less than 50 yards away when the animal was shot. (Detroit, Texas)

Warden Chris Fried pilots the boat as Richards keeps a sharp eye for duck hunters on opening morning at Cooper Lake. (Delta County, Texas)

The heads of three nice buck deer taken illegally by a man without a hunting license. Numerous charges were filed by the local warden. (Dalhart, Texas)

District 1 wardens including Fried (Delta County), Callihan and Newman (Lamar County), Richards (Hunt County), and captain Steve Stapleton take a lunch break after a long morning checking dove hunters near Commerce, Texas.

Feeding time for "unit 1, unit 2, and unit 3". Raising orphaned fawns was a frequent duty over the years.
(Hunt County, Texas)

80

A suspect is questioned after he tried unsuccessfully to out run the warden on foot. The man was carrying over 16,000 dollars all in one-hundred dollar bills inside his pants pockets. (Greenville, Texas)

Standing in an old duck blind he hunted from as a teenager, Richards reflects on his game warden career. This was the last day of patrol. (Wolfe City, Texas)

HOLLYWOOD COMES TO TOWN

WHEN I BECAME A GAME WARDEN I never dreamed I would become famous, it just happened. After many years in the field I was a very well-known state game warden; however, it took a camera crew to put my face in living rooms across America and the world. The thing is, in the beginning I resisted it.

It all started like this. I was driving along a dirt road one morning minding my own business. Then my cell phone made that silly little sound that meant I had just received an email. I hated that sound. Most of the emails I got were useless information coming from some paper pusher in Austin. Anyway, I used my thumb to pull up the message.

Wait a minute. This email was a little different. I began to read about a new TV show that would soon be starting, which would feature Texas State Game Wardens on patrol. Volunteers were requested to let the camera crews ride along on patrol. The email went on to explain that an organizational meeting would be held the next week to let producers and cameramen introduce themselves and answer questions. I stopped reading and again used my thumb to delete what I thought was a stupid idea. I continued on with my day.

A week later my phone rang. It was my captain, Steve Stapleton, on the line. "Hey… did you get that email about the TV show?" he asked.

I replied, "Yeah, but I deleted it."

He said, "I figured you did, but I want you to reconsider." Steve went on to explain that all the wardens who had volunteered to appear on the show were rookies or, at least, very inexperienced. He wanted more seasoned game wardens to represent our area of the state on national TV. After a little more salesmanship, he convinced me to do it.

The next afternoon I was in Rockwall, Texas, at the organizational meeting. What followed was TV history. Within a month, I had a camera crew shadowing me while I was out on patrol. It was a little uncomfortable at first but after a while I forgot the cameras were even there. The more they rode with me, the more comfortable I got. I guess Captain Stapleton knew what he was doing because, being a shit magnet, I was able to give the producers of *Lone Star Law* plenty of material to work with.

The first season aired and I was told it was a hit. The second season and then the third season came and went. By the fourth season my life had changed. Everywhere I went I was recognized. Total strangers would stop me on the street and ask for my autograph or a selfie. Once, my wife and I were in Austin to see a concert at the Frank Erwin Center. As we were waiting at a crosswalk, a gentleman recognized me and said, "Hey Benny, we love your show!" At that point, the crowd around us started looking at me. I guess most of them suddenly recognized me too because they all started cheering and clapping. I will admit it was a good feeling, and at this point I realized *Lone Star Law* was a big deal.

Another time Kristi and I were dogsledding in the back-country of Wyoming. We ran into a group of snowmobilers from Ohio. They recognized me instantly. Requests started coming in from all over asking me to make appearances. My

Facebook fan page lit up with hundreds of comments from fans. In February of 2020 I was asked by a family friend to show up at her restaurant and do a meet and greet. I figured it might stimulate business for her so I agreed. Over five hundred people showed up. WOW!

In the end, being a part of *Lone Star Law* was one of the best experiences of my life. I made lifelong friends along the way. I'm certainly glad my captain asked me to change my mind. It changed my life and my career in many positive ways.

IS THAT HAIR?

MY ACADEMY CLASS graduated on July 31, 1996, but because of all the overtime and comp time we had built up during our training, the class had to take most of the following month off in order to get our hours straight. My first official day in the field came during the last week of August. My captain, Skip McBride, called me up and asked me to drive to the regional office in Mt. Pleasant to pick up a new chip for my radio. Once installed in my radio that chip would give me all the law enforcement channels I would need for the area I would be working in.

At the office Skip and I inserted the new part and tested the radio. The radios we used back then were real dinosaurs compared to the ones in use today. To break a tower or to change to another county frequency, you had to lean over and punch buttons or "dial up a tower." Being my first day, I hadn't had a chance to become familiar with my new radio and I didn't have any of the tower numbers memorized. After Captain McBride gave me some parting advice I headed back to Delta County, anxious to get to work catching outlaws.

About halfway between Mt. Vernon and Sulphur Springs I was cruising down Interstate 30 in the right lane when a small car began to gradually pass me in the left lane. I glanced over and made eye contact with the squirrely looking guy in the passenger seat. As soon as he saw that big baby-blue state seal on the side of my truck his eyes got big and he jerked his head around and said something to the equally squirrely looking driver. This roused my suspicion and my eyes went directly to the steering column. I guess my previous three years of police work at the Richardson Police Department had conditioned me to look for stolen vehicles. I could plainly see there were no keys in the ignition. This was a clue. I allowed the vehicle to pass by in order to check out the license plate. There was not one, not a valid one anyway. The vehicle was displaying an old faded and expired paper buyer's tag. This was a second clue. Now I had seen enough to believe I might be tailing a stolen car.

At this point my new… unfamiliar to me… radio came back into play. I reached down and took the microphone off the hook and punched the button for what I hoped was the Hopkins County channel. As I lifted the microphone to my mouth to call for assistance, I could see the driver checking me out in the rearview mirror. When he saw me talking into the mic he knew the jig was up and he floored it. The chase was on and I was game. I fell in behind the guy at one hundred miles per hour.

My first attempt to contact Hopkins County ended up with me talking to a Titus County dispatcher. The next punch of a button put me in touch with Lamar County… I think. I pitched the microphone in the seat beside me and thought, To hell with it, I don't need any help; I'll take care of this myself. I chased the car all the way to Sulphur Springs before they gave up on outrunning me. A couple of miles before the city limit sign the driver cut hard to the right and took an exit on two wheels. He flew up the exit ramp and turned hard to the left, again on two wheels. He crossed over the interstate, hit the service road on the other side, and then took a gravel road southbound. Everything was happening so fast I didn't get the exit number or the county road number. I had no idea where I was at now, and I knew better than to chase a vehicle into the sticks without letting someone know where I was at. I grabbed the microphone and tried one more time.

I punched in B-8... BINGO! I finally had Hopkins County on the other end of the line. The problem was now trying to tell them where I was. Since I had no road numbers I was reduced to giving them landmarks like barns, colored fence posts, and large tractors sitting in a pasture. Luckily, a veteran officer who knew the area well heard the radio traffic. State Trooper Kenneth Adams cut in advising he knew where I was at and was in route. Now that help was on the way, I again pitched the mic and concentrated on my driving.

The chase down the gravel road got pretty hairy several times. I rounded one curve to find myself traveling southbound with my truck pointing east and west. I jerked the wheel to the right and did a 180-degree spin still headed south. It took me a couple hundred feet of ditch to finally get my truck straight again. All this allowed the bad guys to get a lead on me. However, it didn't last long.

At a Y in the road the driver of the car lost control trying to turn on the loose gravel. He ended up going straight ahead and crashing into a large bois d'arc tree. As I closed in, I saw the driver come out running barefooted. He sailed over a barbed wire fence and disappeared into the brush. The passenger also jumped out running but got hung up in the fence trying to cross it. One of the barbs had a hold of his crotch area and wouldn't let go. I slid up sideways and bailed out on top of him.

About that time Trooper Adams arrived. After handcuffing our suspect, we started our interrogation. The passenger quickly gave us the name of the driver... Bobby

Lee Brooks. Turned out Brooks's vehicle wasn't stolen, it was just a junker. Brooks's car took a bad beating from the tree. A wrecker was summoned to the scene. As Kenneth was filling out an accident report, I peered inside the Nissan at the shattered front windshield. That's when I saw a strange but funny sight. "Hey, look at this, you ain't gonna believe this."

Kenneth looked inside, laughed, and said, "Is that hair?" When Brooks hit the tree his head was thrown into the windshield, which cracked and expanded. When the car came back to a rest, the windshield contracted and pulled several strands of long hair out of his scalp and left them dangling. I walked over to my truck and got an evidence bag. Kenneth asked, "What are you doing?"

I removed the hair from the windshield. Placing the hair in an evidence bag I said, "I'm keeping this in case I need a DNA match." Kenneth just laughed and shook his head.

The reason Brooks was running was because he had a handful of warrants out for his arrest. The next morning the county attorney handed me a new arrest warrant for evading arrest. I took Warden Chris Green on the hunt for Brooks. Chris was stationed in Hopkins County. He knew the area well and was familiar with Brooks. We drove to Brooks's little wooden frame farmhouse near the community of Saltillo. Expecting Brooks might make another run for it, I walked around to the back of the house and got behind the propane tank in the backyard. When Chris rapped on the front door and announced our presence… sure enough… I saw Brooks looking out the back door window. I grabbed my lapel mic and told Chris, "He's in there, I see him." Chris jerked open the front door and shouted, "Come out here, Bobby Lee!" Brooks walked to the front door and surrendered without a fight.

My first two days on the job had been a real hoot. If the rest of my career was anything like this, it was sure to be one heck of a ride.

I'VE GOT PERMISSION

IN DECEMBER OF 2006 deer season was winding down and Lamar County Game Warden Bryan Callihan and I were bored and looking for something to do. We checked a few hunting camps but were unable to stir anything up. So then we decided what the heck, let's stick Surefire up and see if we can catch a road hunter.

We picked a long stretch of Highway 410 south of Detroit, Texas, to set our trap. After strategically placing Surefire in a hay meadow seventy-five yards off the road, I crawled underneath a highway bridge just a short distance away with my handheld radio. Bryan hid in his patrol truck up a dirt road a half mile to the west. An hour or so went by and a few vehicles had passed. A couple of the vehicles honked their horns as they sped down the road. One car stopped and a man got out and whistled then clapped his hands together. Unable to get Surefire to flinch, he got back in and drove away.

More time passed as the sun was getting low on the horizon. I was beginning to think we were going to have a dry run when I heard a vehicle approaching from the north. As the vehicle passed over the bridge where I was hiding, I eased up to the guard railing, where I observed a red Chevy truck pulling a sixteen-foot trailer that carried a four-wheeler. When the truck passed by Surefire, the driver slammed on the brakes, almost causing his truck and trailer to jackknife in the road. After getting his rig stopped the driver inside hesitated for a few seconds and then took off up the hill. I figured he had just stopped for a look and was now leaving but at the top of the hill the driver hit the brakes again. I grabbed my microphone and told Bryan, "I think we've got something."

The truck turned around in the road and headed back. I got back down under the bridge and let my ears tell me what was happening. I expected the driver of the truck to stop again in front of Surefire and shoot. Instead, the truck came down the hill, passed by Surefire, and passed over the bridge. I was confused but stayed put under the bridge. I then heard the truck slow to a stop down the road and begin to turn around again. At this point everything got very quiet. I could no longer hear the truck. I stayed still, listening for any clues as to what was going on up above. After two or three minutes I couldn't stand it any longer, I had to see what was happening.

I slipped out from under the bridge and peeked over the guardrail. I about swallowed my tongue when I saw a man walking down the center of the highway only twenty feet away from me. I'm sure he would have seen me if he had not been so busy jamming .30-06 rounds into his rifle. After the guy passed by, I stepped over the guardrail and quietly fell in behind him walking down the road. I was laughing on the inside as I imagined what I was about to witness.

When the man had closed the distance to within one hundred yards of Surefire, he tiptoed off the road and into the ditch. At the bottom of the ditch he then got down on his hands and knees and began to crawl toward the barbed wire fence that separated him from his prey. All along the way, I was right behind him trying not to bust out in laughter. At the fence the man propped his barrel on the bottom wire, then got down on his belly and prepared to take a shot. At this point it was fairly obvious what the man's intentions were. I had all the evidence I needed. I figured Surefire had enough holes in him and didn't need another. As I saw the man use his thumb to push the safety off on his rifle, I shouted, "What is going on here?"

Like a jack-in-the-box, the man leaped off the ground to his feet. After spinning around to face me he shouted back, "I've got permission!" The following conversation then ensued.

"Permission to do what?"

"Permission to hunt."

"Permission where?"

"On this land."

"On what land?"

"On that land."

"Are you on that land?"

"The deer is."

"Are you sure that's a real deer?"

The man's bottom jaw fell open as he turned and took a good, long look at Surefire still standing motionless in the center of the hay meadow. He turned back to me and said, "I can't believe this, you got me." We then both had a good laugh together. I issued one citation and sent the man on his way.

KEEPING THE WIFE HAPPY

LIKE MOST CALLS my phone rang when I least expected it, and I was on the other side of the county from where the action was taking place. The landowner told me he had heard a shot on the back side of his woods where no one had permission to hunt. He drove around to investigate and located a white pickup truck parked in the ditch beside his fence. With a license plate number in hand, I headed toward the Lydia community in Red River County. The trip would take about thirty minutes and I figured the poacher would be long gone when I showed up. I called my partner Daniel Roraback to see if he might be any closer. He wasn't but told me he would be on his way also.

When I arrived at the location, to my surprise, the white truck was still there with no one around it. I got out and walked around the truck to have a look inside to see if there was any evidence to indicate why it was there. As I was standing in the middle of the oil-top road I heard something coming through the brush over my left shoulder on the opposite side of the fence. I walked to the bottom of the ditch and crouched down just in time to see a man dragging a freshly killed doe through the woods. Now I had no doubt what was going on and why the truck was there. The shot that the rancher had heard over half an hour earlier came from the man's rifle as it was hanging out the window of his truck. After being shot from the roadway, the deer ran for quite a distance through the woods before going down. The poacher followed a blood trail to the location where she lay then field dressed her on the spot. All of this gave me time to get there before the bad guy got away.

Anyway, I stood straight up in full view as the man approached the fence dragging the deer. Upon seeing me, he let go of the deer and dropped his rifle. He then walked straight to me where I met him at the fence. I guess he was not aware that I had seen the deer because he spun a humorous story about looking for a lost dog. With a big smile on my face, I just shook my head from side to side and said, "Not today partner... Now go back and get that deer and make it snappy." Daniel showed up about this time. In the end, I allowed the man to leave with the knowledge that I would be getting a warrant for his arrest. I did, however, seize his rifle and confiscate the dead doe, which Daniel and I loaded into the back of my patrol truck.

This is really where this story begins. After wrapping things up in Lydia Daniel and I decided to cut through the country on back roads to see if we could stir up anything on our way to Clarksville, where we planned to grab some lunch. A few miles down the road, I crested a hilltop. Looking up the roadway, I noticed two men bent over and walking in circles just across the ditch in a pasture. As I slowed to a crawl, I was very curious. The two men appeared to be looking for something. I came up with the theory that they were looking for Indian arrowheads that were commonly found on the hillsides in that area. I pulled up beside the two men and got out with Daniel right behind me.

As we crossed the ditch, the two men greeted us at the edge of the pasture. After shaking our hands, the two men resumed a friendly argument. It seemed that just prior to our arrival one of the men had taken a shot at a doe feeding in that pasture. They had two very different opinions as to whether the deer had been hit. The first hunter explained to us that after he squeezed the trigger the deer leaped high in the air, then stumbled, then ran over the top of the hill. The other hunter just laughed out loud and said, "You know you didn't hit that ole' doe… You never could shoot straight." They both said they were trying to settle the argument by finding a blood trail as we arrived. Daniel and I listened to the two go back and forth about the details of their hunt before the first hunter said, "All I know is my wife is gonna get real suspicious if we don't bring back a deer this time… Every weekend we come up here but I never have anything to show for it."

Upon hearing this, I knew things could not be set up any better. I turned to Daniel and asked, "Well, should we tell them?"

He just stared back at me with a confused look on his face. However, Daniel had worked with me long enough that he could sense that I was up to something so he said, "Sure, go ahead and tell them."

I turned back to the two hunters and said, "Good news guys… I've got your deer in my truck. Follow me."

The four of us hopped the ditch and walked to the back of my truck, where I dropped the tailgate.

At this point, the first hunter turned to the other and shouted, "See, Williard, I did hit that deer!"

The second hunter's mouth fell open as he gazed upon the freshly killed doe lying across the bed of my truck. Daniel was having a hard time trying to keep a straight face so he just walked away. I had an equally hard time keeping a straight face when the first hunter grabbed a front leg and said, "Yep… still limber."

The hunters wanted to know how in the world I found the deer. Thinking they would surely call bullshit, I told them that it had jumped the fence just over the hill, run out into the road, and fell dead in front of my truck. With a toothy grin on his face, the second hunter said to the first one, "Well, I guess your wife will be happy now." "You got that right," came the reply. They bought it hook, line, and sinker.

The two hunters pulled their newfound trophy out of the truck and into the road. We again exchanged handshakes. Daniel and I congratulated them, and then we left the two happy hunters in the road standing over the poor poached deer that I had taken from the poacher earlier. Afterwards, Daniel and I agreed that of all the many confiscated animals that I donated over the years, that doe was put to the best use.

BRUSHY CREEK

WHEN I ARRIVED at my new duty station in Hunt County in the spring of 2013 I quickly discovered there was a sore spot there that would occupy a lot of my time. All the locals referred to the area simply as Brushy Creek. It would be more than two years before I got the area cleaned up and law and order restored. I was told by the farmers and ranchers along Brushy Creek that the trespassing, illegal hunting, and crop destruction by four-wheelers had gotten completely out of hand. Unable to get any help from local law enforcement in the past, they had simply given up trying to stop it. I went to work. I had assured all the landowners in the area that if they were having a problem all they had to do was call me, day or night… and boy… did they ever call me!

One afternoon a farmer called me and said he was hearing gunfire down at the creek. He was concerned someone was on his property shooting near his cattle, and he wanted them off. Brushy Creek actually divided Hunt County from Collin County. Hunt on the east side, Collin on the west side. The dirt road on the Hunt County side that led down to the creek came to a dead end at the creek's edge and picked back up on the opposite side. In years past there was a long wooden bridge there but numerous floods had long since washed it away. Not sure where the gunfire was actually occurring, I approached from the east. Stopping the truck about one hundred yards from Brushy, I got out, locked it up, and started making my way through the tall grass and weeds. Except for the sound of a combine cutting corn in the distance, everything was quiet.

As I neared the edge of the creek on a narrow trail that used to be the county road, the silence was suddenly broken. A very loud shot rang out as a bullet ripped through the tall weeds just to my right. Instinctively, I hit the ground. Then a second loud shot rang out and a second bullet clipped branches of the bois d'arc tree just behind me. This was obviously rifle fire flying by me. The only question now was... is someone trying to kill me?

Not waiting to find out the hard way, I sprang to my feet and charged forward to the creek. I didn't slow down as I pulled my pistol from its holster and ran over the edge, headed straight down. The creek was deep and the bank was very steep so I had a lot of momentum when I reached the bottom. When I reached the water's edge at the bottom of the creek I planted my right foot in an attempt to stop. Something popped in my knee and a lightning bolt of pain shot up my leg. The pain was excruciating but my adrenaline pushed me across to the other side. Then, another rifle shot rang out. Standing upright in the bottom of the creek bed I felt somewhat protected so I began to whistle and yell at the top of my lungs. Some of my words contained four letters. Then there was silence.

After a minute or so I decided to gamble and climbed to the top of the creek bank on the Collin County side. The pain in my knee made the climbing difficult but my focus was on whoever was out there with a rifle. Reaching the top of the bank I found myself back on what was left of the old county road. Just ahead of me I saw what turned out to be a two-foot-by-two-foot cardboard target propped up in the middle of the road. Looking past the bullet-riddled target I saw two men loading rifles into a van. Now I was some kind of pissed. I limped the fifty yards to the van. After a lively ass chewing I issued both men citations for discharging firearms from a public roadway. The two men could see that they could have easily killed another human so they didn't have much to say. I sent the two men on their way and slowly made my way back to the truck.

That afternoon started a long difficult time of recovery. Walking with a very noticeable limp, I had twelve months of doctor's visits and rehab ahead of me. In all my years as a game warden and police officer that close call at Brushy Creek was the nearest I ever came to stopping a bullet.

LET'S JUST SAY WE'RE EVEN

A LIGHT SNOW HAD BEGUN TO FALL when I picked up Erik on the steps of Dalhart Elementary School. We had been planning an afternoon pheasant hunt for several days. I was in such a hurry to get Erik and get out to the cornfields that I forgot to grab his gloves, his heavy coat, and my cell phone. All three items would be badly needed later.

After grabbing a snack at the local convenience store, we headed out of town and made the twenty-mile drive to a spot where I had been seeing a lot of birds feeding the previous week. Erik tinkered with the radio as I kept watching the horizon to the north, as a strong cold front was supposed to arrive soon. When we pulled off the highway onto James Road, a long, dark cloud bank could be seen approaching in the distance. As we drove along the dirt road, nine-year-old Erik began to get excited after we saw several pheasants cross the road in front of us. It was about four o'clock and the temperature was hovering around thirty degrees when our troubles began.

As I rounded a curve I hit a slick spot in the road where a heavy snow from the week before had melted and refrozen. The little S-10 Blazer I was driving slid sideways and headed for the ditch. I overcorrected and ended up in the opposite ditch high-centered in a snowbank. I got out, unconcerned, thinking I could kick a little snow around and get us out. However, after half an hour of digging with my hands, I could see I was fighting a losing battle. My hands were cold and numb and I had gotten nowhere. The realization of the predicament I had gotten us into was like a cold slap in the face. No one knew where we were, I didn't have my phone, we were at least ten miles from the nearest farmhouse, and worst of all, the wind began blowing hard out of the north. December temperatures in the Texas Panhandle can drop thirty or forty degrees in the blink of an eye. Just sitting in the car and waiting on help to come was not an option. It was time to start walking.

I gave my son my big-hooded coat and we started our cold walk as the snowfall picked up. Erik had a hard time keeping up as I walked as fast as I could with my face down to keep the snow and wind out of my eyes. We had covered about two miles when I looked down and found a .20-gauge shotgun hull lying in the road. "Huh… road hunter," I thought to myself as I kept walking. A few minutes later, I heard a gunshot in the distance over my right shoulder. I just kept walking. The only thing I was concerned about was getting my son out of the bitter cold weather brought on by the blue norther that had just arrived with a vengeance.

Suddenly, Erik said, "Daddy, a truck is coming." I spun around, and to my great relief could see a black truck bouncing down the road towards us.

I was the happiest person on earth when the truck pulled up beside us and the man inside asked, "Hey, do y'all need a ride?" At that point, I would have given him everything I owned for a ride.

Erik crawled into the truck, then I got in and slammed the door shut on the old Dodge. Once inside I looked down between my feet. What's this?… Two dead pheasants were lying in the floorboard, along with several empty hulls. I looked over at the driver, who had a .20-gauge shotgun leaning against the seat between his legs. Hmmmm… this could be a problem. The guy hit the gas and down the road we all went.

With a big toothy grin, he said, "It's a good thing I came along… What happened? Did y'all get stuck?"

"Yeah, we did." I then said, "If you're going to Dalhart I sure would appreciate a ride to my house."

"No problem," he replied.

As we made our way down the road, I was pondering whether to say something to the guy about his hunting methods. About that time, a pheasant came out of the ditch and ran across the road in front of us. The guy slammed on his brakes and pointed his shotgun out the window as he pushed the thumb safety off. The rooster flushed, so he wasn't able to get a shot off. Laughing, he pulled the shotgun back inside the window and said, "Well, I'll just have to settle for two today." Erik looked at the man and then looked nervously over at me.

"Do you get a lot of birds that way?" I asked. He just chuckled. "Do you ever worry about getting caught by the game warden?"

He shook his head. "Naw, I ain't ever seen a game warden out here."

We exchanged small talk on the rest of the twenty-minute trip to town.

Once we arrived in Dalhart, I explained to him exactly how to get to my house. About a block from my driveway, the man was telling a story when he stopped in midsentence. He squinted his eyes and his forehead wrinkled up as he studied the green Ford truck parked in my driveway. The same green Ford truck with the state seal of Texas and the words *State*

Game Warden written on the door. You could have heard a pin drop when we pulled up to the curb in front of my house and I got out. I told Erik to go inside as he jumped out of the truck like a rocket.

As I leaned back inside the truck, the man asked, "Are you a game warden?"

Staring at him, I said, "Yep."

"Am I in trouble?"

"Yep."

After a few moments of silence he said, "I don't know what to tell you, sir."

I was very grateful the guy had come along when he did. With that in mind, I said to him, "Mister, as far as I'm concerned, we're even, but this better not happen again… Is it a deal?"

He looked like a new man as he said, "You've got my word on it."

After a handshake he drove away. I hustled inside the house to find a big bowl of hot stew waiting on me. What an afternoon.

CHUNK AND RUN

SHORTLY AFTER MY NEW PARTNER Daniel Roraback graduated the game warden academy and arrived in Red River County, he began prodding me to take him out and stick up Surefire, my decoy deer. I explained to him that timing was everything and he needed to be patient.

After a few months, October finally arrived. On a cool night two weeks before the opening of the deer season, I decided the time was right. Daniel and I took Surefire and met Shawn Hervey up on Highway 44 near the community of Lydia. We stuck the decoy up in the bar ditch on the south side of the highway and hid our trucks in the piney woods directly across the highway.

After an hour or so we hadn't had any traffic come by at all. Daniel started getting antsy and asked several times, "Do you think we'll get him shot?" Shawn and I explained that you never know, but it only takes the right vehicle at the right time.

Just after midnight, the three of us were passing the time with small talk and game warden gossip when the moaning sound of mud-grip tires could be heard approaching in the distance. We continued to listen and then could see the glow of headlights rounding a curve in the road headed our way. "Get ready Daniel, this could be it."

Daniel ran over and jumped behind the wheel of his patrol truck. I slowly walked up to the tree line on the north side of the highway. The truck was traveling pretty fast so I didn't think it was a road hunter. I was wrong. As the big pickup passed by between me and the decoy, the driver slammed on the brakes and shifted into reverse. The truck backed up until the decoy was only twenty feet from the passenger window. I held my breath waiting for a shot.

Four or five seconds passed without anything happening. I decided the occupants were not going to shoot. I figured they simply backed up to look at the deer and would end up honking the horn at it, as happens so many times. I came out of the tree line and started slowly walking toward the truck in order to "shoo" them away. I was about fifteen feet away when... BOOM!! The sound of a rifle going off caused me to fall backwards onto the pavement.

After making sure I wasn't shot, I jumped up and shined my flashlight on the driver. "Game warden... turn off the truck!" The driver just gave me a go-to-hell look and shifted into low gear. Spinning tires indicated they were going to run for it. "Get 'em, Daniel!" I really didn't have to say anything, Daniel was already plowing through the ditch with Hervey right behind him. I looked back up the road to see beer bottles being thrown from the fleeing truck.

By the time I ran across the highway to examine Surefire for bullet holes, Daniel and Shawn were making a felony stop on the truck about a quarter mile up the road. I jogged up the road to get in on the action. When I got there, Shawn told me there was no gun inside the truck.

"Say what?"

I then asked the guy who was the front seat passenger where the rifle was. He said, "We don't have a gun."

I replied, "Look, Junior, that gunshot we heard back there didn't come out of your ass, so where's the gun?" He clammed up and wouldn't say anything else. Shawn and I began walking through the ditches with flashlights, looking for the missing gun. We found it a few yards away. The .308 rifle had been thrown from the moving truck and ended up sticking up in the ditch like a flagpole.

There were five people in the truck. Two young men and a girl who were in the back seat were allowed to take the truck and leave. The driver and front passenger were arrested for hunting deer at night in a vehicle from the roadway. Off to jail we went.

MIRACLE ON TAWAKONI

ASK ANY GAME WARDEN and they will tell you the most challenging situations they ever faced came when they least expected it. The older generation of Texas State Game Wardens were taught from day one that they were on call 24-7-365. Many difficult calls in my career came late at night on my "scheduled" day off. Such was the case one night in the spring of 2018.

Kristi and I had been asleep for over an hour when the cell phone rang on the nightstand beside our bed. When I answered, it was Bowie County Warden Shawn Hervey. I noticed some urgency in his voice as he began to explain to me about information he had just received about an elderly man who was in the water after his boat had capsized on Lake Tawakoni in my county. My first thought was, "Why did Shawn get the call four counties away instead of me?" There was no time to ask questions. Shawn advised the elderly man had been in the water since sunset and wasn't doing good. I threw on a uniform and ran to my patrol truck.

The first thing I did after getting on the road for the thirty-minute drive was call my dispatcher and explain the situation. I asked her to contact the Department of Public Safety and asked for a helicopter to help me in my search. Tawakoni is a huge lake... thirty-nine thousand acres of water. I knew finding this guy in time without help would be almost impossible. I then called my partner, Gary Miller, and got him rolling. On the remainder of the drive down to the lake, I called Shawn Hervey back to get any more information he could give. He didn't have anything new to add but he did explain the unusual circumstances that led to him getting the initial call. As it turned out, the elderly man, after being thrown from his boat, floated in the water for a long time before remembering his cell phone that was in a sandwich bag in the chest pocket of his coveralls. After retrieving his phone, the man called his daughter, who lived in Bowie County, eighty miles away. She, in turn, called the Bowie County Sheriff's Office to plead for help. The sheriff's office called Shawn and then he called me.

As I pulled into the public boat ramp parking lot, a DPS helicopter flew over my head. I made radio contact with it and gave the pilot the best location I could give him to start searching. I had been told the old fisherman was near the center of the lake just north of the two-mile bridge on Highway 276 when he got caught in a thunderstorm with high winds. Gary was waiting with his patrol boat already in the water. The West Tawakoni Fire Rescue Team was also there with two other boats in the water. I grabbed my life vest and a handheld spotlight and ran to the boat. All three boats then pushed away from the ramp and headed out into the darkness. It was a very windy night and the waves were considerable. As we all rounded the first peninsula, the helicopter could be seen near the center of the lake. It was hovering fifty feet above the water shining its spotlight on an object. I was relieved when the pilot came over the radio saying he had located him. We raced to the spot. Once there, all three rescue boats gathered around the V-nose of a fishing boat sticking straight up three feet out of the lake. Floating inside the V-nose, we found our guy. Everyone pitched in and we pulled the shivering man onto the deck of our patrol boat.

At this point, something got my attention. The overpowering smell of gasoline was almost too much to take. It was discovered the man's clothing was soaked with gasoline that had been leaking from the submerged boat's gas tank and collecting under the nose of the boat. He had been floating in the trapped gas for over two hours. I helped him take off his life jacket and we hurried toward the shoreline and a waiting ambulance one mile away. Just before reaching the boat ramp, I was talking to the man trying to gauge his condition. He threw me a huge curve ball when he looked up at me and asked, "Have y'all found my brother yet?"

Say what? Unknown to any of us, there were two men in the boat when it capsized. Things had just really gotten serious. I asked as many questions as I could before paramedics took the man away. Gary and I and the rest of the rescue personnel had a short briefing where I advised them of the additional victim. Time was critically important now. The victim we were looking for now was also elderly and he had been in the sixty-one-degree water for hours. Without a really good location we all fanned out with the agreement to stay in radio contact. Gary and I came up with a plan to go back to the boat and search a line that the prevailing winds would have blown a floating object. We searched and searched for over an hour. I ran through two flashlights and was working on running down a spotlight. With each passing minute we had less and less confidence that we would find him in time. With the cold water, high waves, and wind it would be a miracle if he were still alive.

At 1:00 a.m. with no success, Gary suggested changing our course and making a big circle. That paid off. Five minutes later we were cruising along a stump field when I spotted something bobbing in the water. Gary saw it about the same time I did and throttled up the motor. As we got close I got a better look. IT WAS HIM! As we got even closer I saw movement. HE WAS ALIVE!

Gary positioned the boat with the man at the corner of the transom. He had on a flimsy life jacket that was not fastened and he was bear hugging a five-gallon jug. Full of adrenaline and confidence, I grabbed the man and tried to pull him out of the frigid water and onto the boat. I would have had better luck trying to jump over the moon. I didn't get him two inches out of the water. At this point, he let go of the five-gallon jug he had been holding onto. I yelled to Gary for help. Both of us on our knees, we grabbed the man and pulled in vain. This man was close to three hundred pounds and soaking wet. He was exhausted and unable to help us help him. Gary jumped up and ran to the radio. He spent two or three minutes trying to explain to the other boats where we were. We desperately needed more help but we didn't have the luxury of time to wait.

I told Gary, "We have to get this done now or he is going to die." We both got down on our knees, grabbed clothing as far under the water as we could and began to pull with all the strength we had. We got him halfway into the boat before he hung up on something. I spun around and planted my feet against the motor. Together we pulled once more and we did it. He rolled into our boat. Gary wasted no time in cranking the boat and heading to shore.

At first, the man was very talkative. He was concerned about his brother, which was very understandable. I laid on top of the man trying to keep the cold wind off of him, all the time watching for signs of hypothermia. It didn't take long to notice the signs. He became less talkative and his words became slurred. Then, he began to shake uncontrollably. I feared he would not make it. When we pulled alongside the ramp, Gary tied off as I began to explain to a paramedic that the man's condition was taking a nosedive. I don't know if he didn't realize the importance of what I was telling him or if he was just ignoring me, but he knelt down beside the man lying flat and semiconscious in the bottom of our boat. He then started trying to engage the man in what I felt was ridiculous conversation. Questions like, "How are you doing tonight?" "How are you feeling?" "Can you talk to me?" I sternly told the paramedic, "He doesn't have time for this!" He continued trying to talk to the man and take his pulse.

After another minute or so of the foolishness I jumped out of the boat onto the dock and quickly walked over to a waiting gurney. I grabbed the gurney and pulled it to the side of the boat. I told the paramedic, "Hey, he needs to be in that ambulance now!" I guess everyone around agreed because about six grown men jumped in our boat and lifted the man up and out. The man was quickly put in the ambulance and rushed to the hospital. I backed the trailer into the water and Gary loaded our patrol boat.

Afterwards Gary and I, exhausted, just stood and looked at each other. We were both proud of what we had just accomplished. Those two old fishermen had angels on their shoulders that night... or game wardens, depending on how you look at it. However, being pulled out of the lake wasn't the end of their troubles that night. The first man was treated at the hospital for hypothermia and second-degree chemical burns from his chest down. His brother suffered a serious heart attack after arriving at the hospital. But they both survived.

PASSING THE TEST

I HAVE ALWAYS BEEN A RESTLESS SOUL with a need to know what was on the other side of the hill. In the spring of 2003 I was needing a change of scenery. I had been stationed in one of the smallest counties in Texas for seven years and my work there was done... I wanted out. I requested a transfer to Dalhart, way out in the Texas panhandle. In my younger days, I had worked out in that country on a seismograph crew and wanted another taste of wide-open spaces. After the brass in Austin OK'd my paperwork, the transfer was approved and I was on my way.

Once I arrived at my new duty assignment, I was determined to hit the ground running. I wanted to learn my new country quickly and meet as many of my new landowners as soon as I possibly could. The first few weeks I burned a lot of gas just driving around the county introducing myself to everyone.

One afternoon I was driving up a long, lonely farm-to-market highway near the community of Texline on the border with New Mexico. Way up ahead I noticed an old pickup truck sitting in a pasture near a windmill. As I got closer, I saw an old cowboy counting cattle that were lined up drinking water from the trough at the base of the windmill. I decided I wanted to meet the old gentleman and leave him one of my business cards. Not seeing a gate, I pulled off into the ditch between the highway and the fence. I got out, crawled through the barbed wire, and made my way across the shortgrass prairie, dodging cactus all the way.

As I got within speaking distance, the man stopped what he was doing and walked toward his old farm truck. I watched with interest as the old cowboy, who was dressed in jeans, an old Carhartt shirt, and cowboy boots up to his knees, opened the truck door and reached underneath the seat inside. He came out with an old tin cup in his hand. The cup was partially covered in rust. The part that wasn't rusty was covered in dust.

I spoke up, saying, "Hello, how are you, sir?"

Without saying a word, he took one of his shirttails and ran it around the inside of the cup. He then turned his back and slowly walked over to the windmill. Extending his arm, he held the cup underneath pipe coming up out of the ground from underneath the windmill. Out of the pipe flowed cold, clear groundwater that kept the trough filled for the cattle. Just as the old cup was rusty, so too was the pipe. The last twelve inches of the pipe were covered with a nasty, thick, blackish-green moss. After filling the cup to the brim he turned toward me and asked, "You look thirsty... would you like a drink?"

After a brief staring contest, I could sense there was more going on here than just a water break. Throwing off all my inhibitions about the sanitary value of the cup and the water inside, I went for broke. I took the water-filled cup from him, tilted my head back, and began to drink with gusto. I drank the water from the cup hard and fast. So fast, in fact, some of the water ran down each side of my face. After the cup was empty, I held it out to him and asked, "That's good water... reckon I could get some more?"

After another brief staring contest, a long smile developed across the man's sun-dried face. Finally, he said, "Well, by gosh, it's about time they sent me a real game warden." Then we both busted out in laughter. I took the old man's words to be a very high compliment.

The old cowboy that had tested me that day was seventy-nine-year-old Jerry Lobbley and that afternoon was the beginning of a good friendship. In the weeks that followed our first meeting, Jerry invited me to use his ranch as if it were my own. Thousands of acres of rolling grasslands full of deer, antelope, quail, and pheasant became my personal playground. To this day, whenever I pass through that country on my way to the Rockies, I often think about that cold cup of water.

STOP THAT TAXI

LATE ONE EVENING in early November of 1998 I got a call from an irate landowner in Hopkins County. He told me a truck load of poachers had just shot a buck from the highway near his house. I got the call even though I was stationed in Delta County because Hopkins County had become vacant when Warden Chris Green had transferred over to East Texas. When the landowner called to fill me in on the details of the situation at his ranch, he failed to tell me that he had shot up the suspect's truck with a 7 mm rifle, almost killing the driver and blowing several holes in a four-wheeler in the back. Several days later I would arrest that landowner for his actions.

Anyway, I got on the trail of the road hunters and came up with a name of a suspect from Franklin County. Coincidentally, when I called Franklin County Warden Kevin Davis to ask for his help, he was busy tracking down the same suspect for allegedly killing several other deer that same day. Kevin and I met at the Hopkins County Sheriff's Office after dark and came up with a plan. Rather than wait until the next morning, we decided to go to the suspect's house that night near Mt. Vernon and strike while the iron was still hot.

By the time we got on the interstate headed east it was eleven o'clock. I was following Kevin and we were in a hurry. The interstate traffic was unusually heavy with tractor trailer rigs that night and we were weaving our way through them when we encountered a small, dark-blue, four-door car driving about fifty-five miles per hour in the passing lane. Kevin flashed his bright lights a couple of times in an effort to coax the slow-moving vehicle over to the right lane. After a mile or so Kevin gave up and when there was a small opening between big rigs, he shot around on the right. I moved up now to find my path also blocked by the small car. Over the radio on channel five Kevin said, "Come on around, he ain't gonna move."

I could see Kevin disappearing in the distance as I trailed the slow-moving car. I couldn't get around because of all the traffic quickly passing by in the right lane. I tried what Kevin had tried. I hit my bright lights a couple of times with no response from the driver. Getting a little agitated at this point, I figured what the hell... this is a law enforcement emergency. I then bumped my red and blue emergency lights. There was still no response so now I became concerned. Why wasn't this guy responding to my lights? Why was he driving so much slower than the rest of the traffic? I began to believe that the driver was possibly drunk. Even though I was pursuing a hunting case at the time, in my mind a drunk in hand that I could see was worth two poachers in the bush that I might not ever see. I decided to stop the car and check out the driver.

I again turned on the red and blues and raced up close behind the vehicle. With my headlights illuminating the interior of the car I could see the driver was the only passenger in the front. In the back seat I could see a black man with his head turned around looking at me out the back windshield. This was strange, why wasn't he sitting up front with the driver? After following the vehicle a good distance without any response, I hit the siren. At this point the vehicle moved into the right lane and then onto the shoulder, where it finally stopped just over the county line in Franklin County.

About this time Kevin came back over the radio asking me where I was at. When I told him I had a vehicle stopped, he got a little testy and said, "Come on." I got out and carefully walked to the driver's side door, where I was surprised to find out the vehicle I had stopped was actually a poorly marked taxi cab. I identified myself and the driver greeted me with a strong Jamaican accent. The register on the dash showed the passenger had rung up a $155 bill so far. Hmmmm… now who pays that much for a taxi ride?

After a few questions I determined the driver wasn't drunk but he had some interesting information. I found out he had picked up his rider at the Extended Stay motel on Greenville Avenue in Dallas and was taking him to Texarkana, 177 miles away. Oh, really? My attention now turned to the passenger in the back seat. He was a black gentleman that looked to be about twenty-five or thirty. I noticed he refused to make eye contact with me and instead stared out the passenger side window. The longer I stood beside the taxi asking questions, the lower he sank into the back seat. Now my common sense, street smarts, and police experience kicked in. There was little doubt in my mind what was going on here.

I asked the driver to get out and meet at the back of the vehicle. After getting his consent, the driver popped the trunk lid and let me examine the stuff inside. I saw a large suitcase and a big green army-type duffel bag. I asked the driver who the luggage belonged to, and he said his passenger had loaded all of it into the trunk when picked up in Dallas. I leaned inside and ran my hand down the side of the duffel bag where, through the canvas, I felt a very hard object about two feet long. I told the driver to stay put and I walked back to my truck. I grabbed the microphone and called Kevin to ask him to get in contact with the county K-9 officer. Kevin quickly retorted, "Come on, man… we ain't got time for this."

Now it was my time to get testy over the radio. I didn't have any patience with anyone I considered a rookie questioning anything I did. "Kevin, if you got a K-9 officer in this county, I need him right here… right now!"

I guess Kevin now knew I had something. "Ok… I'll get him and we'll be right there."

About five minutes later Kevin pulled up and parked on the service road about twenty yards away. To my dismay, the black Labrador retriever he habitually carried with him bailed out of his truck, ran to the taxi cab, and began running around it. I knew there were drugs in the taxi, which meant someone was going to jail, which meant I was going to court. I didn't want to explain to a defense attorney and a jury why I had two different dogs running around that night. "Kevin, get this dog out of here!" Kevin grabbed his dog by the collar, dragged him to his truck, and locked him inside.

At that very moment, K-9 officer Chris Mars pulled up behind me and got out. I told Officer Mars what I had. I told him what my suspicions were and turned the cab over to him. He ran his German shepherd around the cab a couple of times before the big dog jumped up inside the trunk and began feverishly biting and clawing the suitcase. Mars leaned inside and began unzipping the luggage. I could see the black man in the back passenger seat was now sitting upright and taking a great interest in what was going on in the trunk as he peered out the back windshield.

As Kevin and I held our breath in anticipation, Mars suddenly stood up, turned around, and barked, "He's carrying drugs… pop him." Assuming someone transporting a large amount of drugs might be armed, I drew my weapon and ordered the man out of the taxi. He and the driver were both taken into custody.

Over the next half hour, we transported the pair to jail and had the taxi towed to the sheriff's office where it could be searched further. At the jail, numerous bundles of marijuana and four large PVC tubes filled with powdered cocaine were discovered inside the luggage. Something very interesting happened next.

At the jail I received a phone call from a special agent with the Drug Enforcement Agency. After identifying himself he asked me who I had in custody. When I told him who I had, he told me to put my suspect in a cell alone and not let anyone talk to him. The agent then told me he was on his way to my location from Dallas and hung up the phone. To this day, I have no idea how he knew I had arrested my suspect, nor how he found out so fast. Sure enough, about an hour and a half later two agents in business suits showed up and took charge of the dope and the investigation. I was relieved. It was more dope than I had ever seized and I didn't need the paperwork.

After leaving the jail Kevin and I could have high-fived each other and called it a night. Instead, we got back on our original track and headed to our poacher's house. Arriving at around two o'clock in the morning, we rustled him out of bed. We didn't have to ask too many questions before he started confessing his sins. When the sun came up a few hours later, we had seized a quarter-million dollars' worth of narcotics and a three-buck deer. Not a bad night at all.

Five months later, Kevin and I found ourselves in federal court testifying over the drug arrest. The defendant's high-priced defense attorney had gotten the court to agree to a suppression hearing. I spent over an hour on the stand being grilled about every single word I spoke and every move I made on the night in question. Unbelievably, when it was over the court held that the defendant's rights to privacy had been violated when I squeezed the outside of his duffel bag without his permission. Excuse the hell out of me! The charges against him were thrown out and he walked. Are you kidding me? Well, at least he walked without his dope. From that day on I knew the so-called War on Drugs was simply a myth.

TWISTER

SPRINGTIME IN TEXAS can be very nice or not so nice depending on how far off the nearest thunderstorm is. During my career as a game warden I had a front-row seat to some really nasty weather. Tornadoes in Canton, Garland, DeKalb, Lancaster... I was at all of them within minutes of them passing through. However, it was one small tornado back in 1999 that could have gotten me admitted to a local hospital quicker than any of them.

I was out on a stormy day patrolling near the small community of Emblem in Hopkins County. The area was under several weather warnings, so I was listening to the radio for any info from storm spotters. Around 10:00 a.m. the Commerce Police Department reported a tornado on the ground north of Commerce headed east. That put the tornado on a path to pass right over my head. I drove to the top of a big hill on Highway 71 and sat looking west over the Sulphur River bottoms. After a few minutes I could see it coming. The sky darkened and turned a pale green color. Then it started to hail.

I was about to turn around in the highway and run when a white Ford Mustang drove around me and headed down the hill into the bottom toward the twister. I knew I had to stop the people in the vehicle and warn them. I hit the red and blue lights and pulled them over. When I jumped out of the truck I was almost blown to the ground by the wind. I ran to the driver's window and yelled to the woman driving, "There is a tornado coming, you need to turn around!" She didn't need to hear anything else. She spun around in the road and peeled out. I got back in my truck and did likewise. An hour or so later, after the storm passed, I heard a lot of damage had been done in Sulphur Springs, so I went to check it out. It turned out to be a pretty powerful storm.

Fast-forward two weeks later… My wife and I were out for a drive enjoying one of the few days that I got off work. We decided to drive through Doctor's Creek Park at Cooper Lake. As we pulled up to the office, we were greeted by Park Ranger Glen Stone. "Hello Benny, how are y'all today?"

"Good, Glen, what have you got going today?" I replied. This is the point where things got complicated and almost dangerous for me.

Glen said, "Hey, I'm glad you're here, because two young women came by earlier and left some flowers and candy for you."

Confused, I asked, "Are you sure they're for me?"

Nodding his head in the affirmative he said, "Yeah, they said give them to the game warden, I guess that's you."

Very nervously, I looked over at my wife Kristi. I never had seen that strange look in her eyes before, or since. Her eyes had gone from a lovely shade of brown to jet black. Her hair, especially the hair on the back of her neck, seemed to stand up a little differently. She was no longer just sitting at the other end of the seat. She was now coiled up at the other end of the seat, ready to strike. But it was that crooked little grin, yes that crooked little "I gotcha" grin, that sent chills up my spine. At a loss for words, I told Glen that I would be right inside to get the flowers and candy. Kristi quickly corrected me by advising that "WE" would be right in to get the flowers and candy.

Walking into the park office, I saw a big bouquet of beautiful flowers and a box of chocolates, along with a small, gift-wrapped box. Kristi spied the card attached to the flowers and extracted it with a forceful jerk. She began tearing into the envelope like a kid would tear into a Christmas present, but with a totally different kind of enthusiasm. I just stood there trying to figure out what woman would have possibly sent me flowers and candy. Heck, I had known a few girls back in college, but that was long, long ago.

As Kristi silently read the card, I prepared myself for the death sentence she would surely impose. But wait… As she read on I noticed the evil expression on her face lightened just a little. The lines on her forehead went away, and her teeth didn't seem so long and sharp. After a couple more seconds, she sniggered, smiled, and handed me the card.

Confused more than ever, I quickly skimmed over the card myself. Sweet relief! As it turned out, the card was from the woman driving the white Ford Mustang during the storm two weeks earlier. In the card she explained that when I stopped her she was on her way home with her daughter. She wrote that after the storm passed, she went back home to find it totally destroyed. Nothing was left but the concrete slab. She stated that if I had not stopped her, she would have been pulling up in her driveway when the twister hit and she and her daughter would have been hurt or killed. The flowers and candy were her way of saying, "Thank you." And oh yeah, the gift-wrapped box contained a VHS video of the movie *Twister*.

I was certainly glad I survived that twister and its aftermath. Without that card to explain things, I would have been in the middle of a really bad storm, indeed.

KIDS DO THE DARNDEST THINGS

IT WAS ABOUT ONE O'CLOCK in the morning when the phone rang. On the other end of the line was a rancher in Delta County who reported hearing three shots near one of his wheat fields. He went on to explain that he felt like someone was spotlighting deer on his property. I felt like he was probably right so I got up, threw on my uniform, and headed out into the dark night.

It took me about twenty minutes to get to the area near the community of Kensing. The particular piece of property where the shots reportedly came from bordered another large tract of land that sat on the banks of the South Sulphur River, which was running bank full due to the heavy rains the week before. With my headlights turned off, I drove up the dirt road that passed by all the properties in that area. I didn't see any vehicles moving around so I began checking gates. Sure enough I found a closed gate that was "dummy locked." This was unusual since the gate was almost always locked unless the owner of the deer camp located on the property was around. I also noticed several sets of fresh tire tracks in the soft mud underneath the gate. I blocked the gate with my truck to prevent anyone getting out. I then walked in to check the deer camp in the woods just over the crest of a hill.

As I walked through the dark woods I looked up through the treetops at millions of stars overhead in a crystal-clear night sky. The temperature then was just about at the freezing mark. As I topped the hill I could see the glow of a fire at the camp. I also could now hear laughter. Arriving silently at the camp, I stood behind a pickup truck and counted nine young people standing around the campfire. Eight boys and one girl. A few feet away from the group I saw a shotgun leaning against a tree. I figured I had now located the source of the shots but wanted to hear a full confession. I thought that if I listened long enough someone in the group would start talking about whatever it was they had been shooting at.

It was difficult to hear clearly what was being said, for a couple of reasons. First, the sound of floodwater rushing down the Sulphur River was making a low roaring noise in the distance. Second, I was simply too far away and needed to get closer to the campfire. I got down on my hands and knees and slowly crawled along the ground to a stack of cordwood only ten feet from the group standing in a circle around the fire. Once in position behind the stack of wood, I rolled over onto my back, stretched out, and began to listen. What a treat I was in for.

For the next twenty minutes I heard some real juicy gossip about a whole bunch of teenagers in Cooper, Texas. The party around the fire continued with everyone getting a chance to tell a good story, until one of the boys in the group upped the ante. He began suggesting that the girl in the group show everyone her chest. However, he didn't use the word *chest* when he made his suggestion.

Now I was really in a pickle. If I stood up and announced my presence now, it would have been said that the talk of bare breasts stirred me into action. On the other hand, if I didn't stand up and say something and just stayed hidden, I might be accused of trying to get a look along with the other boys. Either way it was a dicey situation. There was a third option. I could have simply crawled away into the night and forgot the whole matter, but that wasn't going to happen. I decided to just remain still and quiet. The other boys joined in with the first, trying to coax the girl into a peep show. A few seconds later the hooting and hollering from the boys suggested to me that they must have gotten their look.

Things calmed back down as I continued to lie on the ground. I was now freezing to death and starting to cramp up. I decided they were not going to say anything about hunting, and I had had enough. Now I was looking for the right time to get up and surprise the teenagers. I didn't have to wait long. As one young man was in the middle of a good story, another guy turned around and picked up a log off the stack of wood about three feet from my head. He quickly turned around and shouted, "Look out!" He pitched the log into the center of the campfire which caused hot coals and embers to fly out in all directions. Everyone jumped back to avoid being burned.

This was the opportunity I was waiting for. I quickly stood up and walked around the stack of wood and took my place in the circle as everyone gathered back around the fire. Wearing my felt cowboy hat, I'm sure I had a big grin on my face as I reached out my hands to warm them against the fire. I went completely unnoticed as the guy on the other side of the fire resumed telling his story.

A few seconds went by before the storyteller stopped in midsentence and pointed his finger at me across the fire. "Who are you?" he asked.

At this point the two guys on either side looked at me and jumped back. One of them said, "Holy shit... where did you come from?"

I announced to the group that I was the game warden of Delta County. All the boys became suddenly quiet, but not the girl. She immediately started asking me how long I had been here. She must have asked me a half dozen times how long I had been at the deer camp before I looked at her and said, "Long enough to know something very personal about you." When she heard that she grabbed a blanket off a lawn chair, wrapped it around herself, and went inside the camp house.

I then got back to business and asked the boys about the shots that had been reported to me. One of the young men explained that he had just completed basic training and was home on leave from the Air Force. He also said he had gotten a new shotgun for Christmas and had been shooting it at beer cans earlier. I was able to find three empty hulls lying on the ground near the gun still leaning against the tree. The case was solved. When the boys at the camp realized they were not in any kind of trouble, they became a lot more talkative. One of them asked, "How did you hear our shots?" It was now my time to have some fun.

Standing in the center of the boys, I told them that I had heard the shots as I was going upriver in my boat.

All the boys' mouths fell open, eyes got wide, and then almost in unison they asked, "What are you doing in a boat on the river at night?"

My reply... "I am looking for outlaws killing deer at night."

"But the river is flooded," another one said.

I shrugged my shoulders, "Yeah I know... I have to be careful around those log jams."

Another question from the group: "How long do you stay out there?"

I explained, "Well I usually just spend the night!"

Another question: "Where do you sleep?"

I summed up, "In a barn if I can find one. If not I may have to get under a hollow log."

Now the boys all fell silent again. They just looked at me with blank stares. I sensed that they had bought what I had just told them... hook, line, and sinker. In their minds I was no longer just a common man, but rather some kind of backwoods swamp creature that needed to be avoided. Bidding them farewell I turned away from the group and headed toward the river at a slow jog. I turned my flashlight on every fifty yards or so to prove I went to the river. At the river I made a big circle back to my truck, got in, and quietly drove away.

Over the next few years I got a lot of mileage out of that little episode in the camp that night. Teenagers in Delta County never really looked at me the same after that.

THE FIRST AND THE LAST

I GRADUATED THE TEXAS GAME WARDEN ACADEMY in Austin on July 31, 1996. My department gave my class the next thirty-one days off to get settled into our new duty stations. Landing in Delta County, I hit the ground running. I began looking for a temporary home for my family. My options for rental homes were pretty slim. We ended up in an old frame home in Enloe, Texas. That little white home served as my base of operations for the first five months of my career.

My first official day checking hunters in the field fell on September 1… the opening day of dove season. As I remember, that morning was a little slow. I checked numerous hunters but didn't uncover any violations. I was a new rookie game warden so I will admit that I was eager to put some ink on paper. It didn't take long for things to heat up. I got word from Delta County dispatch advising me of a call they had just received concerning a man in a white pickup shooting doves off utility lines just west of Cooper. With the suspect's license plate number written across the palm of my hand I headed to town. At the big intersection in Cooper I was about to turn west on Highway 64 when I spotted a white pickup that matched the description of the suspect vehicle. I got behind it and yes… the plates matched the suspect vehicle was looking for. I hit the red and blues and pulled the pickup over at the edge of town.

As I walked up to the driver's side door there was a shotgun lying across the passenger seat. I also spotted two spent hulls up on the dashboard. I asked the young man driving to step out of the truck. As he exited, I could see two freshly killed doves lying in the floorboard between his feet... BINGO! I now had all the evidence I needed. I collected his hunting license and driver's license and explained why I had him stopped. At first he wanted to argue over the matter until I explained that a witness had turned him in and was willing to testify. There was nothing to do now but complete some paperwork. I could have arrested him but I used some discretion. I issued two citations: the first for hunting migratory birds from a vehicle and the second for discharging a firearm from the roadway. After seizing the illegally taken birds, I sent him on his way. As it turned out, the young man I cited was the grandson of the local justice of the peace, who would preside over the cases I was about to file. I was off to a great start with the local politicians.

And that was it. I had just issued my first citation as a Texas State Game Warden. It would be followed by thousands of other citations and many, many arrests. I was a street cop before becoming a warden so I was no stranger to writing tickets and putting handcuffs on people. However, as the years went by, I found that I was less and less inclined to pull out my ticket book. Looking at the "big picture" and the uneven way judges dealt with violators caused me to issue a lot of warnings late in my career. I never did lose my enthusiasm for putting stupid, drunk, mean, or selfish people in jail. Especially if they liked to run their mouth.

Being a game warden is dangerous, especially the way I approached it. I figured it out early that the worst violators of the law did their dirty deeds under the cover of darkness late at night. So that was my favorite time to work. Those many late nights I spent patrolling paid off. During my career I investigated a large variety of crimes. Of course there were the wildlife crimes but also home burglaries, cattle thefts, stolen cars, dope dealers by the dozens, and violent family assaults. I even filed a case once in Red River County for arson. That particular case sticks out in my mind.

I was hidden one late night in the northern part of that county. I was watching a lonely stretch of Highway 410 waiting for a spotlighter to come by and take a shot at a small herd of deer nearby. About 2:00 a.m. a Jeep Cherokee stopped in the highway just to my left. Using the available moonlight I watched through binoculars as the driver got out and walked over to a row of large bales of hay stacked beside the road against the fence line. To my amazement one of the bales of hay suddenly went up in flames. Startled, I turned on my lights and came out of my hiding spot. The driver ran back to the Jeep and tore ass.

I had a choice. I could give chase or put out the fire. I decided on the latter. Grabbing a fire extinguisher out of my toolbox, I ran to the fire and luckily got it under control and put out. After getting back in the truck I grabbed the microphone and called for a deputy. As luck would have it, a deputy was just down the road in Woodland. I advised him of the situation and told him to block the highway there. A few minutes later he had my arsonist stopped. Upon my arrival I found out the driver was a woman well known to law enforcement, and her boyfriend in the passenger seat had just been released from prison. Anyway, I arrested her and headed to the jail in Clarksville. To show her displeasure with me, she pissed in the passenger seat. I never did get the smell out of that truck seat. She got hers though. Two years later she was shot dead by another woman over a man.

Looking back I guess the most serious investigation I ever headed up started out as a hunting accident that was reported to me. During my initial investigation of that situation things just didn't add up. I had a man lying dead in an open pasture from a gunshot wound to the chest. After collecting all the evidence and talking to all available witnesses I wondered… "How could this be an accident?" Over the course of three weeks the investigation took a dark turn and ended up with me, the Red River County sheriff, and a Texas Ranger serving a search warrant on a home. There we uncovered a rifle hidden in a barn in the property. A family member of the dead man was later charged with several crimes related to the death of the victim. That same family member attempted suicide during the investigation. It was a tragic turn of events that I will never forget.

I don't know if I had angels on my shoulders, I was just lucky, or I was very good at what I did for a living. Maybe it was a combination of all three. But in all my years as a game warden I was never seriously injured and never was forced to seriously injure anyone else. I credit that to three things: my verbal skills, my attitude, and my reputation.

It didn't take me too long to get a reputation amongst outlaws. Early in my career the word spread that this warden wasn't putting up with any crap. My attitude was "I didn't get into law enforcement to make friends… My job was to enforce the law." My verbal skills and my unique way of explaining things to criminals left no room for misinterpretation. If faced with a situation late at night on a back road with a potentially uncooperative, violent subject, there was a blueprint I followed. I would explain things in a way that would leave no doubt in that person's mind about the tidal wave of violence that he was about to experience if things turned physical between the two of us. Over the course of my career very few men tested me after I explained things. Those who did ended up behind bars one way or another. Don't get me wrong. I always tried to be friendly and kind when I was allowed to be. My personal guideline was "Be friendly, be fair, but be firm."

The end came suddenly and unexpectedly. Late on a Sunday afternoon I was patrolling at the municipal lake near the city limits of Greenville. It was a cold, rainy day so there were not many people fishing. However, I did see a small car parked on the levee near the spillway. From past experience I assumed someone was using a net to take fish in the overflow at the base of the dam. As I pulled up to the car, sure enough a Hispanic man carrying a net popped up in the weeds on the back of the dam. He was accompanied by a young boy. Upon seeing me the man turned around and started walking away. I exited my truck and whistled to the man. After getting his attention, I motioned to him to come back to the top of the dam. I met him and the boy at the back of their car.

It didn't take long for me to determine the man didn't speak a lick of English. He was from El Salvador. I assumed he was in the country illegally but didn't raise that issue. Using the young boy as an interpreter, I asked the man for a fishing license. He had no fishing license. I asked the man for a driver's license. He had no driver's license. I made my decision quickly. I issued one citation and one warning. Since I didn't actually see the man using the net, he received a warning for fishing without a license. However, I issued him a citation for driving without a valid driver's license. Yes, it is true that I didn't actually see him drive the car to the lake, but I was certain the boy hadn't driven it out there. After he signed the citation I sent them on their way. Just like that, it was over. I had just issued the last citation I would ever issue as a game warden.

The next week a situation arose that effectively put an end to my career and changed the country forever. A virus, known as COVID-19, spread quickly around the globe. To stop the spread of the disease in Texas, Governor Abbott issued orders that restricted travel across the state. Field wardens were told that until further notice we were no longer in a law enforcement mode but rather a disaster response mode.

It was during the height of this pandemic that I made a decision that I had been struggling with. I decided that after a quarter century of service, it was time for me to retire and ride off into the sunset. It was over. My work was done. On May 12, 2020, I pulled into my driveway at my home and parked my truck. I sat quietly for a few moments before reaching down and removing the radio mic from the console. Then I spoke those familiar words that I had spoken so many times before.

"2119 County... I'm 10-7."

CPSIA information can be obtained
at www.ICGtesting.com
Printed in the USA
BVHW040458160222
629094BV00001B/1